GOD IN THE DOCK

Born in Ireland in 1898, C. S. Lewis was educated at Malvern College for a year and then privately. He gained a triple First at Oxford and was a Fellow and Tutor at Magdalen College 1925–54. In 1954 he became Professor of Medieval and Renaissance Literature at Cambridge. He was an outstanding and popular lecturer and had a deep and lasting influence on his pupils.

C. S. Lewis was for many years an atheist, and described his conversion in *Surprised by Joy*: 'In the Trinity Term of 1929 I gave in, and admitted that God was God ... perhaps the most dejected and reluctant convert in all England.' It was this experience that helped him to understand not only apathy but active unwillingness to accept religion, and, as a Christian writer, gifted with an exceptionally brilliant and logical mind and a lucid, lively style, he was without peer. *The Problem of Pain, The Screwtape Letters, Mere Christianity, The Four Loves* and the posthumous *Prayer: Letters to Malcolm* are only a few of his best-selling works. He also wrote books for children, and some science fiction, besides many works of literary criticism. His works are known to millions of people all over the world in translation. He died on 22 November 1963, at his home in Oxford.

D1147280

BOOKS BY C. S. LEWIS
AVAILABLE FROM FOUNT PAPERBACKS

The Abolition of Man
The Business of Heaven
Christian Reflections
Christian Reunion
Compelling Reason
The Dark Tower
Fern-seed and Elephants
The Four Loves
The Great Divorce
Letters
Letters to Children
Mere Christianity
Miracles
Narrative Poems
The Pilgrim's Regress
Poems
Prayer: Letters to Malcolm
The Problem of Pain
Readings for Reflection and Meditation
Reflections on the Psalms
The Screwtape Letters
Screwtape Proposes a Toast
Surprised by Joy
Till We Have Faces

BOOKS FOR CHILDREN
AVAILABLE FROM HARPERCOLLINS

The Chronicles of Narnia

C. S. Lewis

GOD IN THE DOCK

Essays on Theology

EDITED BY

WALTER HOOPER

Fount

An Imprint of HarperCollins*Publishers*

Fount F is an Imprint of
HarperCollins*Religious*
Part of HarperCollins*Publishers*
77–85 Fulham Palace Road, London w6 8jb

First published in Great Britain
in 1971 by Geoffrey Bles
This edition published in 1998 by Fount Paperbacks

2   3   4   5   6   7   8   9   10

Text Copyright © 1971, 1979 C. S. Lewis Pte

Preface Copyright © 1979 Walter Hooper

Walter Hooper asserts the moral right to be
identified as the editor of this work

A catalogue record for this book
is available from the British Library

ISBN 0 00 628088 9

Printed and bound in Great Britain by
Caledonian International Book Manufacturing Ltd, Glasgow

CONDITIONS OF SALE
All rights reserved. No part of this publication may be reproduced,
stored in a retrieval system, or transmitted, in any form or by any means,
electronic, mechanical, photocopying, recording or otherwise, without
the prior permission of the publishers.

This book is sold subject to the condition that it shall not, by way of trade
or otherwise, be lent, re-sold, hired out or otherwise circulated without the
publisher's prior consent in any form of binding or cover other than that
in which it is published and without a similar condition including this
condition being imposed on the subsequent purchaser.

Contents

Preface

C. S. Lewis is one writer of this century of whom the Greek epigram about Plato seems eminently exact: 'In whatever direction we go, we meet him on the way back.' He was unique in arguing for truth and following an argument to its logical conclusion. It is probably this – inseparable from his supreme clarity – which has caused him to be regarded as one who understood more of what Christianity is about than many who busy themselves with little else.

One need look no further than the essay 'Myth Became Fact', for there he strides all the pitfalls in which writhe so many modern writers, including the unbelievers who thought recently to astonish us with their *Myth of God Incarnate* (1977). Indeed, compared to Lewis theirs is a tiresome lot. So often is 'myth' nowadays used as a synonym for 'lie' or – at best – a kind of picture-language for savages. How tedious have our contemporaries become: even in his wild, atheistical youth Lewis had got as far as that, for in a letter of 12 October 1916 he wrote to one of his oldest friends, Arthur Greeves:

All religions, that is, all mythologies to give them their proper name, are merely man's own invention ... Thus religion, that is to say mythology, grew up. Often too, great men were regarded as gods after their death – such as Heracles or Odin: thus after the death of a Hebrew philosopher Yeshua (whose name we have corrupted into Jesus) he became regarded as a god, a cult sprang up, which was afterwards connected with the ancient Hebrew Jahweh-worship, and so Christianity came into being – one mythology among many.

Latter-day scholars might have found an ally in him had he stopped there: but Lewis continued arguing with himself, thinking very hard about 'myth', by which he meant similar instances of an event (such as a dying god who is revived) found among many religions. The answer he had been seeking came on the evening of 19 September 1931 when he invited J. R. R. Tolkien and Hugo Dyson to dine with him in Magdalen College. The talk went on all night long: in Lewis's rooms and down by the trees of Addison's Walk where the wind was wild. Wild, too, were the thoughts going through Lewis's mind. Indeed, this same night he defined myth as 'breathing a lie through silver'. Before the morning he was converted. Writing to Greeves shortly afterwards, he said:

What Dyson and Tolkien showed me was this: that if I met the idea of sacrifice in a Pagan story I didn't mind it at all: again, that if I met the idea of a god sacrificing himself to himself ... I liked it very much and was mysteriously moved by it: again, that the idea of the dying and reviving god (Balder, Adonis, Bacchus) similarly moved me provided I met it anywhere except *in the Gospels ... Now the story of Christ is simply a true myth: a myth working on us in the same way as the others, but with this tremendous difference that* it really happened.

It was Lewis's belief that if many of the professional theologians, instead of sitting on the fence, had expounded Christianity to the people there there would have been no need for him. As it was, he was forced by his own conscience to do all he could to supply that most desperate of needs: for it was clear to him that while 'There is nothing in the nature of the younger generation which incapacitates them for receiving Christianity' it is nevertheless true that 'no generation can bequeath to its successors what it has not got'.

His task would have been easier if modernist theologians never wrote anything. Still, while they, with their apostasy and cant, often prompted Lewis to write, his permanent motivation was an unswerving love for God and those whom the Shepherd came to save. For this he gave so freely, both of his time and income. Where did he find the time? During the course of his remarkable apostolate as a defender of full-blooded, supernatural Christianity he never shirked any task. 'That part of the line,' he said, 'where I thought I could serve best was also the part that seemed to be thinnest. And to it I naturally went.'

Lewis has been found to be more prophetic than even his own generation gave him credit for. Another timely essay in this book, 'Priestesses in the Church?', will be anathema to those modernist bishops and others who have aligned themselves with the World and who forget that what they regard as 'guidance' can come from somewhere other than Heaven.

Indeed all the essays in this book were aimed at defending orthodox Christianity – especially the miraculous elements in the Faith which, if removed, bring down the whole fabric of belief. They are reprinted from, and represent about half the contents of, Lewis's *Undeceptions: Essays on Theology and Ethics* (1971). But their original appearances go back further:

1 'Miracles' was preached in St Jude on the Hill Church, London, and appeared in *St Jude's Gazette*, No. 73 (October 1942) pp. 4–7. A shorter and slightly altered version of this sermon was published in *The Guardian* (2 October 1942) p. 316.

2 'Dogma and the Universe' was published in two parts in *The Guardian* (19 and 26 March 1943) pp. 96, 104, 107.

3 'Myth Became Fact' first appeared in *World Dominion*, vol. XXII (September-October 1944) pp. 267–70.

4 'Religion and Science' is reprinted from *The Coventry Evening Telegraph* (3 January 1945) p. 4.

5 'The Laws of Nature' is also from *The Coventry Evening Telegraph* (4 April 1945) p. 4.

6 'The Grand Miracle' was preached in St Jude on the Hill Church, London, and was afterwards published in *The Guardian* (27 April 1945) pp. 161, 165.

7 'Man or Rabbit?' was originally published as a pamphlet by the Student Christian Movement in Schools. It is not dated, but it probably appeared in 1946.

8 'The Trouble with "X" ...' was first published in the *Bristol Diocesan Gazette*, vol. XXVII (August 1948) pp. 3–6.

9 'What Are We to Make of Jesus Christ?' is reprinted from *Asking Them Questions*, Third Series, ed. Ronald Selby Wright (Oxford University Press, 1950) pp. 95–104.

10 'Must Our Image of God Go?' is taken from *The Observer* (24 March 1963) p. 14.

11 'Priestesses in the Church?' was originally published as 'Notes on the Way' in *Time and Tide*, vol. XXIX (14 August 1948) pp. 830–31.

12 'God in the Dock' is my title for 'Difficulties in Presenting the Christian Faith to Modern Unbelievers', *Lumen Vitae*, vol. III (September 1948) pp. 421–6.

13 'We Have No "Right to Happiness"' is the last thing Lewis wrote before his death in November 1963, and it appeared shortly afterwards in *The Saturday Evening Post*, vol. CCXXXVI (21–28 December 1963) pp. 10, 12.

For those who regard their reading as 'fashionable' here's a book they won't enjoy. But the fault does not lie with the book. As Lewis has said, 'All that is not eternal is eternally out of date.' The rapid passing of 'sensational' and 'up-to-date' books ought to be sufficient warning that unless one takes those sensible words to heart one might easily flit past the very thing one has, hopefully, set out to find.

Walter Hooper
Oxford, August 1978

Miracles
(1942)

I have known only one person in my life who claimed to have seen a ghost. It was a woman; and the interesting thing is that she disbelieved in the immortality of the soul before seeing the ghost and still disbelieves after having seen it. She thinks it was a hallucination. In other words, seeing is not believing. This is the first thing to get clear in talking about miracles. Whatever experiences we may have, we shall not regard them as miraculous if we already hold a philosophy which excludes the supernatural. Any event which is claimed as a miracle is, in the last resort, an experience received from the senses; and the senses are not infallible. We can always say we have been the victims of an illusion; if we disbelieve in the supernatural this is what we always shall say. Hence, whether miracles have really ceased or not, they would certainly appear to cease in Western Europe as materialism became the popular creed. For let us make no mistake. If the end of the world appeared in all the literal trappings of the Apocalypse,[1] the modern materialist saw with his own eyes

---

[1] The Book of Revelation.

the heavens rolled up[2] and the great white throne appearing,[3] if he had the sensation of being himself hurled into the Lake of Fire,[4] he would continue forever, in that lake itself, to regard his experience as an illusion and to find the explanation of it in psycho-analysis, or cerebral pathology. Experience by itself proves nothing. If a man doubts whether he is dreaming or waking, no experiment can solve his doubt, since every experiment may itself be part of the dream. Experience proves this, or that, or nothing, according to the preconceptions we bring to it.

This fact that the interpretation of experience depends on preconceptions, is often used as an argument against miracles. It is said that our ancestors, taking the supernatural for granted and greedy of wonders, read the miraculous into events that were really not miracles. And in a sense I grant it. That is to say, I think that just as our preconceptions would prevent us from apprehending miracles if they really occurred, so their preconceptions would lead them to imagine miracles even if they did not occur. In the same way, the doting man will think his wife faithful when she is not and the suspicious man will not think her faithful when she is: the question of her actual fidelity remains meanwhile to be settled, if at all, on other grounds. But there is one thing often said about our ancestors which we must *not* say. We must not say 'They believed in miracles because they did not know the laws of nature.' This is nonsense. When St Joseph discovered that his bride was pregnant, he was 'minded

[2] Ibid., 6:14.
[3] Ibid., 20:11.
[4] Ibid., 19:20; 20:10, 14–15; 21:8.

to put her away'.[5] He knew enough biology for that. Otherwise, of course, he would not have regarded pregnancy as a proof of infidelity. When he accepted the Christian explanation, he regarded it as a miracle precisely because he knew enough of the laws of nature to know that this was a suspension of them. When the disciples saw Christ walking on the water they were frightened:[6] they would not have been frightened unless they had known the laws of nature and known that this was an exception. If a man had no conception of a regular order in nature, then of course he could not notice departures from that order: just as a dunce who does not understand the normal metre of a poem is also unconscious of the poet's variations from it. Nothing is wonderful except the abnormal and nothing is abnormal until we have grasped the norm. Complete ignorance of the laws of nature would preclude the perception of the miraculous just as rigidly as complete disbelief in the supernatural precludes it, perhaps even more so. For while the materialist would have at least to explain miracles away, the man wholly ignorant of nature would simply not notice them.

The experience of a miracle in fact requires two conditions. First we must believe in a normal stability of nature, which means we must recognize that the data offered by our senses recur in regular patterns. Secondly, we must believe in some reality beyond nature. When both beliefs are held, and not till then, we can approach with an open mind the various reports which claim that this super- or extra-natural reality has sometimes invaded and disturbed the sensuous content of space and time

---

[5] Matthew 1:19.
[6] Matthew 14:26; Mark 6:49; John 6:19.

which makes our 'natural' world. The belief in such a super-natural reality itself can neither be proved nor disproved by experience. The arguments for its existence are metaphysical, and to me conclusive. They turn on the fact that even to think and act in the natural world we have to assume something beyond it and even assume that we partly belong to that something. In order to think we must claim for our own reasoning a validity which is not credible if our thought is merely a function of our brain, and our brains a by-product of irrational physical processes. In order to act, above the level of mere impulse, we must claim a similar validity for our judgements of good and evil. In both cases we get the same disquieting result. The concept of nature itself is one we have reached only tacitly by claiming a sort of *super*-natural status for ourselves.

If we frankly accept this position and then turn to the evidence, we find, of course, that accounts of the supernatural meet us on every side. History is full of them – often in the same documents which we accept wherever they do not report miracles. Respectable missionaries report them not infrequently. The whole Church of Rome claims their continued occurrence. Intimate conversation elicits from almost every acquaintance at least one episode in his life which is what he would call 'queer' or 'rum'. No doubt most stories of miracles are unreliable; but then, as anyone can see by reading the papers, so are most stories of all events. Each story must be taken on its merits: what one must not do is to rule out the supernatural as the one impossible explanation. Thus you may disbelieve in the Mons Angels[7]

[7] Lewis is referring to the story that angels appeared, protecting British troops in their retreat from Mons, France, on 26 August 1914. A recent summary of the event by Jill Kitson, 'Did Angels appear to British troops at Mons?' is found in *History Makers*, No. 3 (1969), pp. 132–3.

because you cannot find a sufficient number of sensible people who say they saw them. But if you found a sufficient number, it would, in my view, be unreasonable to explain this by collective hallucination. For we know enough of psychology to know that spontaneous unanimity in hallucination is very improbable, and we do not know enough of the supernatural to know that a manifestation of angels is equally improbable. The supernatural theory is the less improbable of the two. When the Old Testament says that Sennacherib's invasion was stopped by angels,[8] and Herodotus says it was stopped by a lot of mice who came and ate up all the bowstrings of his army,[9] an open-minded man will be on the side of the angels. Unless you start by begging the question, there is nothing intrinsically unlikely in the existence of angels or in the action ascribed to them. But mice just don't do these things.

A great deal of scepticism now current about the miracles of Our Lord does not, however, come from disbelief of all reality beyond nature. It comes from two ideas which are respectable but I think mistaken. In the first place, modern people have an almost aesthetic dislike of miracles. Admitting that God can, they doubt if He would. To violate the laws He Himself has imposed on His creation seems to them arbitrary, clumsy, a theatrical device only fit to impress savages – a solecism against the grammar of the universe. In the second place, many people confuse the laws of nature with the laws of thought and imagine that their reversal or suspension would be a contradiction in terms – as if the resurrection of the dead were the same sort of thing as two and two making five.

[8] 2 Kings 19:35.
[9] Herodotus, Bk. II, Sect. 141.

I have only recently found the answer to the first objection. I found it first in George MacDonald and then later in St Athanasius. This is what St Athanasius says in his little book *On the Incarnation*: 'Our Lord took a body like to ours and lived as a man in order that those who had refused to recognize Him in His superintendence and captaincy of the whole universe might come to recognize from the works He did here below in the body that what dwelled in this body was the Word of God.' This accords exactly with Christ's own account of His miracles: 'The Son can do nothing of Himself, but what He seeth the Father do.'[10] The doctrine, as I understand it, is something like this:

There is an activity of God displayed throughout creation, a wholesale activity let us say which men refuse to recognize. The miracles done by God incarnate, living as a man in Palestine, perform the very same things as this wholesale activity, but at a different speed and on a smaller scale. One of their chief purposes is that men having seen a thing done by personal power on the small scale, may recognize, when they see the same thing done on the large scale, that the power behind it is also personal – is indeed the very same person who lived among us two thousand years ago. The miracles in fact are a retelling in small letters of the very same story which is written across the whole world in letters too large for some of us to see. Of that larger script part is already visible, part is still unsolved. In other words, some of the miracles do locally what God has already done universally: others do locally what he has not yet done, but will do. In that sense, and from our human point of view, some are reminders and others prophecies.

[10] John 5:19.

God creates the vine and teaches it to draw up water by its roots and, with the aid of the sun, to turn that water into a juice which will ferment and take on certain qualities. Thus every year, from Noah's time till ours, God turns water into wine. That, men fail to see. Either like the Pagans they refer the process to some finite spirit, Bacchus or Dionysus: or else, like the moderns, they attribute real and ultimate causality to the chemical and other material phenomena which are all that our senses can discover in it. But when Christ at Cana makes water into wine, the mask is off.[11] The miracle has only half its effect if it only convinces us that Christ is God: it will have its full effect if whenever we see a vineyard or drink a glass of wine we remember that here works He who sat at the wedding party in Cana. Every year God makes a little corn into much corn: the seed is sown and there is an increase, and men, according to the fashion of their age, say 'It is Ceres, it is Adonis, it is the Corn King,' or else 'It is the laws of nature.' The close-up, the translation, of this annual wonder is the feeding of the five thousand.[12] Bread is not made there of nothing. Bread is not made of stones, as the Devil once suggested to Our Lord in vain.[13] A little bread is made into much bread. The Son will do nothing but what He sees the Father do. There is, so to speak, a family *style*. The miracles of healing fall into the same pattern. This is sometimes obscured for us by the somewhat magical view we tend to take of ordinary medicine. The doctors themselves do not take this view. The magic is not in the medicine but in the patient's body.

[11] John 2:1–11.
[12] Matthew 14:15–21; Mark 6:34–44; Luke 9:12–17; John 6:1–11.
[13] Matthew 4:3; Luke 4:3.

What the doctor does is to stimulate nature's functions in the body, or to remove hindrances. In a sense, though we speak for convenience of healing a cut, every cut heals itself; no dressing will make skin grow over a cut on a corpse. That same mysterious energy which we call gravitational when it steers the planets and biochemical when it heals a body is the efficient cause of all recoveries, and if God exists, that energy, directly or indirectly, is His. All who are cured are cured by Him, the healer within. But once He did it visibly, a Man meeting a man. Where He does not work within in this mode, the organism dies. Hence Christ's one miracle of destruction is also in harmony with God's wholesale activity. His bodily hand held out in symbolic wrath blasted a single fig tree;[14] but no tree died that year in Palestine, or any year, or in any land, or even ever will, save because He has done something, or (more likely) ceased to do something, to it.

When He fed the thousands he multiplied fish as well as bread. Look in every bay and almost every river. This swarming, pulsating fecundity shows He is still at work. The ancients had a god called Genius – the god of animal and human fertility, the presiding spirit of gynaecology, embryology, or the marriage bed – the 'genial bed' as they called it after its god Genius.[15] As the miracles of wine and bread and healing showed who Bacchus really was, who Ceres, who Apollo, and that all were one, so this miraculous multiplication of fish reveals the real Genius. And with that we stand at the threshold of the miracle which for some reason most offends modern ears. I can understand the

---

[14] Matthew 21:19; Mark 11:13–20.
[15] For further information on this subject see the chapter on 'Genius and Genius' in Lewis's *Studies in Medieval and Renaissance Literature*, ed. Walter Hooper (Cambridge, 1966), pp. 169–74.

man who denies the miraculous altogether; but what is one to make of the people who admit some miracles but deny the Virgin Birth? Is it that for all their lip service to the laws of nature there is only one law of nature that they really believe? Or is it that they see in this miracle a slur upon sexual intercourse which is rapidly becoming the one thing venerated in a world without veneration? No miracle is in fact more significant. What happens in ordinary generation? What is a father's function in the act of begetting? A microscopic particle of matter from his body fertilizes the female: and with that microscopic particle passes, it may be, the colour of his hair and his great grandfather's hanging lip, and the human form in all its complexity of bones, liver, sinews, heart, and limbs, and prehuman form which the embryo will recapitulate in the womb. Behind every spermatozoon lies the whole history of the universe: locked within it is no small part of the world's future. That is God's normal way of making a man – a process that takes centuries, beginning with the creation of matter itself, and narrowing to one second and one particle at the moment of begetting. And once again men will mistake the sense impressions which this creative act throws off for the act itself or else refer it to some finite being such as Genius. Once, therefore, God does it directly, instantaneously; without a spermatozoon, without the millenniums of organic history behind the spermatozoon. There was of course another reason. This time He was creating not simply a man, but the man who was to be Himself: the only true Man. The process which leads to the spermatozoon has carried down with it through the centuries much undesirable silt; the life which reaches us by that normal route is tainted. To avoid that taint, to give humanity a fresh start, He once short-circuited the process. There is a vulgar anti-God paper which some anonymous donor sends me every week. In it recently I saw the taunt that we Christians believe in a God who committed adultery with the wife of a Jewish carpenter. The answer to that is that if you describe the action of God in fertilizing Mary as 'adultery', then, in that sense, God would have committed adultery with every woman who ever had a baby. For what He did once without a human father, He does always even when He uses a human father as His instrument. For the human father in ordinary generation is only a carrier, sometimes an unwilling carrier, always the last in a long line of carriers, of life that comes from the supreme life. Thus the filth that our poor, muddled, sincere, resentful enemies fling at the Holy One, either does not stick, or, sticking, turns into glory.

So much for the miracles which do small and quick what we have already seen in the large letters of God's universal activity. But before I go on to the second class – those which foreshadow parts of the universal activity we have not yet seen – I must guard against a misunderstanding. Do not imagine I am trying to make the miracles less miraculous. I am not arguing that they are more probable because they are less unlike natural events: I am trying to answer those who think them arbitrary, theatrical, unworthy of God, meaningless interruptions of universal order. They remain in my view wholly miraculous. To do instantly with dead and baked corn what ordinarily happens slowly with live seed is just as great a miracle as to make bread of stones. Just as great, but a different *kind* of miracle. That is the point. When I open Ovid,[16] or Grimm, I find the sort of miracles which really would be arbitrary. Trees talk, houses turn into trees, magic rings

[16] The reference is to Ovid's (43 BC–AD 18) *Metamorphoses*.

raise tables richly spread with food in lonely places, ships become goddesses, and men are changed into snakes or birds or bears. It is fun to read about: the least suspicion that it had really happened would turn that fun into nightmare. You find no miracles of that kind in the Gospels. Such things, if they could be, would prove that some alien power was invading nature; they would not in the least prove that it was the same power which had made nature and rules her every day. But the true miracles express not simply a god, but God: that which is outside nature, not as a foreigner, but as her sovereign. They announce not merely that a King has visited our town, but that it is *the* King, *our* King.

The second class of miracles, on this view, foretell what God has not yet done, but will do, universally. He raised one man (the man who was Himself) from the dead because He will one day raise all men from the dead. Perhaps not only men, for there are hints in the New Testament that all creation will eventually be rescued from decay, restored to shape and subserve the splendour of re-made humanity.[17] The Transfiguration[18] and the walking on the water[19] are glimpses of the beauty and the effortless power over all matter which will belong to men when they are really waked by God. Now resurrection certainly involves 'reversal' of natural process in the sense that it involves a series of changes moving in the opposite direction to those we see. At death, matter which has been organic, falls back gradually into the inorganic, to be finally scattered and used perhaps in other

---

[17] E.g. Romans 8:22: 'We know that the whole creation groaneth and travaileth in pain together until now.'
[18] Matthew 17:1–9; Mark 9:2–10.
[19] Matthew 14:26; Mark 6:49; John 6:19.

organisms. Resurrection would be the reverse process. It would not of course mean the restoration to each personality of those very atoms, numerically the same, which had made its first or 'natural' body. There would not be enough to go round, for one thing; and for another, the unity of the body even in this life was consistent with a slow but perplexed change of its actual ingredients. But it certainly does mean matter of some kind rushing towards organism as now we see it rushing away. It means, in fact, playing backwards a film we have already seen played forwards. In that sense it is reversal of nature. But, of course, it is a further question whether reversal in this sense is necessarily contradiction. Do we know that the film cannot be played backwards?

Well, in one sense, it is precisely the teaching of modern physics that the film never works backwards. For modern physics, as you have heard before, the universe is 'running down'. Disorganization and chance are continually increasing. There will come a time, not infinitely remote, when it will be wholly run down or wholly disorganized, and science knows of no possible return from that state. There must have been a time, not infinitely remote, in the past when it was wound up, though science knows of no winding-up process. The point is that for our ancestors the universe was a picture: for modern physics it is a story. If the universe is a picture these things either appear in that picture or not; and if they don't, since it is an infinite picture, one may suspect that they are contrary to the nature of things. But a story is a different matter; specially if it is an incomplete story. And the story told by modern physics might be told briefly in the words 'Humpty Dumpty was falling.' That is, it proclaims itself an incomplete story. There must have been a time before he fell, when he was sitting on the wall; there must be a time after he has reached the ground. It is quite true that science knows of no horses and men who can put him together again once he has reached the ground and broken. But then she also knows of no means by which he could originally have been put on the wall. You wouldn't expect her to. All science rests on observation: all our observations are taken *during* Humpty Dumpty's fall, because we were born after he lost his seat on the wall and shall be extinct long before he reaches the ground. But to assume from observations taken while the clock is running down that the unimaginable winding-up which must have preceded this process cannot occur when the process is over is the merest dogmatism. From the very nature of the case the laws of degradation and disorganization which we find in matter at present, cannot be the ultimate and eternal nature of things. If they were, there would have been nothing to degrade and disorganize. Humpty Dumpty can't fall off a wall that never existed.

Obviously, an event which lies outside the falling or disintegrating process which we know as nature, is not imaginable. If anything is clear from the records of Our Lord's appearances after His resurrection, it is that the risen body was very different from the body that died and that it lives under conditions quite unlike those of natural life. It is frequently not recognized by those who see it:[20] and it is not related to space in the same way as our bodies. The sudden appearances and disappearances[21] suggest the ghost of popular tradition: yet He emphatically insists that He is not merely a spirit and takes steps to demonstrate that

[20] Luke 24:13–31, 36–7; John 20:14–16.
[21] Mark 16–14; Luke 24:31, 36; John 20:19, 26.

the risen body can still perform animal operations, such as eating.[22] What makes all this baffling to us is our assumption that to pass beyond what we call nature – beyond the three dimensions and the five highly specialized and limited senses – is immediately to be in a world of pure negative spiritually, a world where space of any sort and sense of any sort have no function. I know no grounds for believing this. To explain even an atom Schrödinger wants seven dimensions: and give us new senses and we should find a new nature. There may be natures piled upon natures, each supernatural to the one beneath it, before we come to the abyss of pure spirit; and to be in that abyss, at the right hand of the Father, may not mean being absent from any of these natures – may mean a yet more dynamic presence on all levels. That is why I think it very rash to assume that the story of the Ascension is mere allegory. I know it sounds like the work of people who imagined an absolute up and down and a local heaven in the sky. But to say this is after all to say 'Assuming that the story is fake, we could thus explain how it arose.' Without that assumption we find ourselves 'moving about in worlds unrealized'[23] with no probability – or improbability – to guide us. For if the story is true then a being still in some mode, though not our mode, corporeal, withdrew at His own will from the Nature presented by our three dimensions and five senses, not necessarily into the non-sensuous and undimensioned but possibly into, or through, a world or worlds of super-sense and super-space. And He might choose to do it gradually. Who on earth knows what the spectators might see? If they

[22] Luke 24:42–3; John 21:13.
[23] This is probably a misquotation of Wordsworth's 'Moving about in worlds not realized'. *Intimations of Immortality*, ix, 149.

say they saw a momentary movement along the vertical plane – then an indistinct mass – then nothing – who is to pronounce this improbable?

My time is nearly up and I must be very brief with the second class of people whom I promised to deal with: those who mistake the laws of nature for laws of thought and, therefore, think that any departure from them is a self-contradiction, like a square circle or two and two making five. To think this is to imagine that the normal processes of nature are transparent to the intellect, that we can say why she behaves as she does. For, of course, if we cannot see why a thing is so, then we cannot see any reason why it should not be otherwise. But in fact the actual course of nature is wholly inexplicable. I don't mean that science has not yet explained it, but may do so some day. I mean that the very nature of explanation makes it impossible that we should even explain why matter has the properties it has. For explanation, by its very nature, deals with a world of 'ifs and ands'. Every explanation takes the form 'Since A, therefore B' or 'If C, then D'. In order to explain any event you have to assume the universe as a going concern, a machine working in a particular way. Since this particular way of working is the basis of all explanation, it can never be itself explained. We can see no reason why it should not have worked a different way.

To say this is not only to remove the suspicion that miracle is self-contradictory, but also to realize how deeply right St Athanasius was when he found an essential likeness between the miracles of Our Lord and the general order of nature. Both are a full stop for the explaining intellect. If the 'natural' means that which can be fitted into a class, that which obeys a norm, that which can be paralleled, that which can be explained by reference to other events, then nature herself as a whole is *not* natural. If a miracle means that which must simply be accepted, the unanswerable actuality which gives no account of itself but simply *is*, then the universe is one great miracle. To direct us to that great miracle is one main object of the earthly acts of Christ: they are, as He Himself said, Signs.[24] They serve to remind us that the explanations of particular events which we derive *from* the given, the unexplained, the almost wilful character of the actual universe, are not explanations of that character. These Signs do not take us away from reality; they recall us to it – recall us from our dream world of 'ifs and ands' to the stunning actuality of everything that is real. They are focal points at which more reality becomes visible than we ordinarily see at once. I have spoken of how He made miraculous bread and wine and of how, when the Virgin conceived, He had shown Himself the true Genius whom men had ignorantly worshipped long before. It goes deeper than that. Bread and wine were to have an even more sacred significance for Christians and the act of generation was to be the chosen symbol among all mystics for the union of the soul with God. These things are no accidents. With Him there are no accidents. When He created the vegetable world He knew already what dreams the annual death and resurrection of the corn would cause to stir in pious Pagan minds, He knew already that He Himself must so die and live again and in what sense, including and far transcending the old religion of the Corn King. He would say 'This is my Body.'[25] *Common* bread, miraculous bread, sacramental bread – these three are distinct, but not to be

[24] Matthew 12:39; 16:4; 24:24, 30; Mark 13:22; 16:17, 20; Luke 21:11, 25.
[25] Matthew 26:26; Mark 14:22; Luke 22:19; 1 Corinthians 11:24.

separated. Divine reality is like a fugue. All His acts are different, but they all rhyme or echo to one another. It is this that makes Christianity so difficult to talk about. Fix your mind on any one story or any one doctrine and it becomes at once a magnet to which truth and glory come rushing from all levels of being. Our featureless pantheistic unities and glib rationalist distinctions are alike defeated by the seamless, yet ever-varying, texture of reality, the liveness, the elusiveness, the intertwined harmonies of the multi-dimensional fertility of God. But if this is the difficulty, it is also one of the firm grounds of our belief. To think that this was a fable, a product of our own brains as they are a product of matter would be to believe that this vast symphonic splendour had come out of something much smaller and emptier than itself. It is not so. We are nearer to the truth in the vision seen by Julian of Norwich, when Christ appeared to her holding in His hand a little thing like a hazel nut and saying, 'This is all that is created.'[26] And it seemed to her so small and weak that she wondered how it could hold together at all.

---

[26] *Sixteen Revelations of Divine Love*, ed. Roger Hudleston (London, 1927), ch. 5, p. 9.

2

Dogma and the Universe
(1943)

It is a common reproach against Christianity that its dogmas are unchanging, while human knowledge is in continual growth. Hence, to unbelievers, we seem to be always engaged in the hopeless task of trying to force the new knowledge into moulds which it has outgrown. I think this feeling alienates the outsider much more than any particular discrepancies between this or that doctrine and this or that scientific theory. We may, as we say, 'get over' dozens of isolated 'difficulties', but that does not alter his sense that the endeavour as a whole is doomed to failure and perverse: indeed, the more ingenious, the more perverse. For it seems to him clear that, if our ancestors had known what we know about the universe, Christianity would never have existed at all: and, however we patch and mend, no system of thought which claims to be immutable can, in the long run, adjust itself to our growing knowledge.

That is the position I am going to try to answer. But before I go on to what I regard as the fundamental answer, I would like to clear up certain points about the actual relations between Christian doctrine and the scientific knowledge we already have. That is a different matter from the continual growth of knowledge we imagine, whether rightly or wrongly, in the future and which, as some think, is bound to defeat us in the end.

In one respect, as many Christians have noticed, contemporary science has recently come into line with Christian doctrine, and parted company with the classical forms of materialism. If anything emerges clearly from modern physics, it is that nature is not everlasting. The universe had a beginning, and will have an end. But the great materialistic systems of the past all believed in the eternity, and thence in the self-existence of matter. As Professor Whittaker said in the Riddell Lectures of 1942, 'It was never possible to oppose seriously the dogma of the Creation except by maintaining that the world has existed from all eternity in more or less its present state.'[1] This fundamental ground for materialism has now been withdrawn. We should not lean too heavily on this, for scientific theories change. But at the moment it appears that the burden of proof rests, not on us, but on those who deny that nature has some cause beyond herself.

In popular thought, however, the origin of the universe has counted (I think) for less than its character – its immense size and its apparent indifference, if not hostility, to human life. And very often this impresses people all the more because it is supposed to be a modern discovery – an excellent example of those things which our ancestors did not know and which, if they had known them, would have prevented the very beginnings of Christianity. Here there is a simple historical falsehood. Ptolemy knew just as well as Eddington[2] that the earth was infinitesimal

---

[1] Sir Edmund Taylor Whittaker, *The Beginning and End of the World*, Riddell Memorial Lectures, Fourteenth Series (Oxford, 1942), p. 40.
[2] Sir Arthur Stanley Eddington (1882–1944).

in comparison with the whole content of space.[3] There is no question here of knowledge having grown until the frame of archaic
thought is no longer able to contain it. The real question is why
the spatial insignificance of the earth, after being known for
centuries, should suddenly in the last century have become an
argument against Christianity. I do not know why this has happened; but I am sure it does not mark an increased clarity of
thought, for the argument from size is, in my opinion, very feeble.

When the doctor at a post-mortem diagnoses poison, pointing
to the state of the dead man's organs, his argument is rational
because he has a clear idea of that opposite state in which the
organs would have been found if no poison were present. In the
same way, if we use the vastness of space and the smallness of
earth to disprove the existence of God, we ought to have a clear
idea of the sort of universe we should expect if God did exist.
But have we? Whatever space may be in itself – and, of course,
some moderns think it finite – we certainly perceive it as three-
dimensional, and to three-dimensional space we can conceive no
boundaries. By the very forms of our perceptions, therefore, we
must feel as if we lived somewhere in infinite space. If we discovered no objects in this infinite space except those which are
of use to man (our own sun and moon), then this vast emptiness
would certainly be used as a strong argument against the existence of God. If we discover other bodies, they must be habit-
able or uninhabitable: and the odd thing is that both these
hypotheses are used as grounds for rejecting Christianity. If the
universe is teeming with life, this, we are told, reduces to absurdity the Christian claim – or what is thought to be the Christian

---

[3] Ptolemy lived at Alexandria in the second century AD. The reference is to his
Almagest, Bk. I, ch. 5.

claim – that man is unique, and the Christian doctrine that to this one planet God came down and was incarnate for us men and our salvation. If, on the other hand, the earth is really unique, then that proves that life is only an accidental by-product in the universe, and so again disproves our religion. Really, we are hard to please. We treat God as the police treat a man when he is arrested; whatever He does will be used in evidence against Him. I do not think this is due to our wickedness. I suspect there is something in our very mode of thought which makes it inevitable that we should always be baffled by actual existence, *whatever* character actual existence may have. Perhaps a finite and contingent creature – a creature that might not have existed – will always find it hard to acquiesce in the brute fact that it is, here and now, attached to an actual order of things.

However that may be, it is certain that the whole argument from size rests on the assumption that differences of size ought to coincide with differences of value: for unless they do, there is, of course, no reason why the minute earth and the yet smaller human creatures upon it should not be the most important things in a universe that contains the spiral nebulae. Now, is this assumption rational or emotional? I feel, as well as anyone else, the absurdity of supposing that the galaxy could be of less moment in God's eyes than such an atom as a human being. But I notice that I feel no similar absurdity in supposing that a man of five-feet high may be more important than another man who is five-feet three and a half – nor that a man may matter more than a tree, or a brain more than a leg. In other words, the feeling of absurdity arises only if the differences of size are very great. But where a relation is perceived by reason it holds good universally. If size and value had any real connection, small differences in size would accompany small differences in value as surely as large differences in size accompany large differences in value. But no sane man could suppose that this is so. I don't think the taller man *slightly* more valuable than the shorter one. I don't allow a slight superiority to trees over men, and then neglect it because it is too small to bother about. I perceive, as long as I am dealing with the small differences of size, that they have no connection with value whatsoever. I therefore conclude that the importance attached to the great differences of size is an affair, not of reason but of emotion – of that peculiar emotion which superiorities in size produce only after a certain point of absolute size has been reached.

We are inveterate poets. When a quantity is very great, we cease to regard it as mere quantity. Our imaginations awake. Instead of mere quantity, we now have a quality – the sublime. Unless this were so, the merely arithmetical greatness of the galaxy would be no more impressive than the figures in a telephone directory. It is thus, in a sense, from ourselves that the material universe derives its power to over-awe us. To a mind which did not share our emotions, and lacked our imaginative energies, the argument from size would be sheerly meaningless. Men look on the starry heavens with reverence: monkeys do not. The silence of the eternal spaces terrified Pascal,[4] but it was the greatness of Pascal that enabled them to do so. When we are frightened by the greatness of the universe, we are (almost literally) frightened by our own shadows: for these light years and billions of centuries are mere arithmetic until the shadow of man, the poet, the maker of myth, falls upon them. I do not say

[4] Blaise Pascal, *Pensées*, No. 206.

we are wrong to tremble at his shadow; it is a shadow of an image of God. But if ever the vastness of matter threatens to overcross our spirits, one must remember that it is matter spiritualized which does so. To puny man, the great nebula in Andromeda owes in a sense its greatness.

And this drives me to say yet again that we are hard to please. If the world in which we found ourselves were not vast and strange enough to give us Pascal's terror, what poor creatures we should be! Being what we are, rational but also animate, amphibians who start from the world of sense and proceed through myth and metaphor to the world of spirit, I do not see how we could have come to know the greatness of God without that hint furnished by the greatness of the material universe. Once again, what sort of universe do we demand? If it were small enough to be cosy, it would not be big enough to be sublime. If it is large enough for us to stretch our spiritual limbs in, it must be large enough to baffle us. Cramped or terrified, we must, in any conceivable world, be one or the other. I prefer terror. I should be suffocated in a universe that I could see to the end of. Have you never, when walking in a wood, turned back deliberately for fear you should come out at the other side and thus make it ever after in your imagination a mere beggarly strip of trees?

I hope you do not think I am suggesting that God made the spiral nebulae solely or chiefly in order to give me the experience of awe and bewilderment. I have not the faintest idea why He made them; on the whole, I think it would be rather surprising if I had. As far as I understand the matter, Christianity is not wedded to an anthropocentric view of the universe as a whole. The first chapters of Genesis, no doubt, give the story of creation in the form of a folk-tale – a fact recognized as early as the time of St Jerome – and if you take them alone you might get that impression. But it is not confirmed by the Bible as a whole. There are few places in literature where we are more sternly warned against making man the measure of all things than in the Book of Job: 'Canst thou draw out leviathan with an hook? Will he make a covenant with thee? Wilt thou take him for a servant? Shall not one be cast down even at the sight of him?'[5] In St Paul, the powers of the skies seem usually to be hostile to man. It is, of course, the essence of Christianity that God loves man and for his sake became man and died. But that does not prove that man is the sole end of Nature. In the parable, it was the one lost sheep that the shepherd went in search of:[6] it was not the only sheep in the flock, and we are not told that it was the most valuable – save in so far as the most desperately in need has, while the need lasts, a peculiar value in the eyes of Love. The doctrine of the Incarnation would conflict with what we know of this vast universe only if we knew also that there were other rational species in it who had, like us, fallen, and who needed redemption in the same mode, and that they had not been vouchsafed it. But we know none of these things. It may be full of life that needs no redemption. It may be full of life that has been redeemed. It may be full of things quite other than life which satisfy the Divine Wisdom in fashions one cannot conceive. We are in no position to draw up maps of God's psychology, and prescribe limits to His interests. We would not do so even for a man whom we knew to be greater than ourselves. The doctrine that God is Love and that

[5] Job 41:1, 4, 9.
[6] Matthew 18:12; Luke 15:4.

24

He delights in men, are positive doctrines, not limiting doctrines. He is not less than this. What more He may be, we do not know; we know only that He must be more than we can conceive. It is to be expected that His creation should be, in the main, unintelligible to us.

Christians themselves have been much to blame for the misunderstanding on these matters. They have a bad habit of talking as if revelation existed to gratify curiosity by illuminating all creation so that it becomes self-explanatory and all questions are answered. But revelation appears to me to be purely practical, to be addressed to the particular animal, Fallen Man, for the relief of his urgent necessities – not to the spirit of inquiry in man for the gratification of his liberal curiosity. We know that God has visited and redeemed His people, and that tells us just as much about the general character of the creation as a dose given to one sick hen on a big farm tells us about the general character of farming in England. What we must do, which road we must take to the fountain of life, we know, and none who has seriously followed the directions complains that he has been deceived. But whether there are other creatures like ourselves, and how they are dealt with: whether inanimate matter exists only to serve living creatures or for some other reason: whether the immensity of space is a means to some end, or an illusion, or simply the natural mode in which infinite energy might be expected to create – on all these points I think we are left to our own speculations.

No. It is not Christianity which need fear the giant universe. It is those systems which place the whole meaning of existence in biological or social evolution on our own planet. It is the creative evolutionist, the Bergsonian or Shavian, or the Communist, who should tremble when he looks up at the night sky. For he really is committed to a sinking ship. He really is attempting to ignore the discovered nature of things, as though by concentrating on the possibly upward trend in a single planet he could make himself forget the inevitable downward trend in the universe as a whole, the trend to low temperatures and irrevocable disorganization. For entropy is the real cosmic wave, and evolution only a momentary tellurian ripple within it.

On these grounds, then, I submit that we Christians have as little to fear as anyone from the knowledge actually acquired. But, as I said at the beginning, that is not the fundamental answer. The endless fluctuations of scientific theory which seem today so much friendlier to us than in the last century may turn against us tomorrow. The basic answer lies elsewhere.

Let me remind you of the question we are trying to answer. It is this: How can an unchanging system survive the continual increase of knowledge? Now, in certain cases we know very well how it can. A mature scholar reading a great passage in Plato, and taking in at one glance the metaphysics, the literary beauty, and the place of both in the history of Europe, is in a very different position from a boy learning the Greek alphabet. Yet through that unchanging system of the alphabet all this vast mental and emotional activity is operating. It has not been broken by the new knowledge. It is not outworn. If it changed, all would be chaos. A great Christian statesman, considering the morality of a measure which will affect millions of lives, and which involves economic, geographical and political considerations of the utmost complexity, is in a different position from a boy first learning that one must not cheat or tell lies, or hurt innocent people. But only in so far as that first knowledge of the great moral platitudes survives unimpaired in the statesman will his deliberation be moral at all. If that goes, then there has been no progress, but only mere change. For change is not progress unless the core remains unchanged. A small oak grows into a big oak; if it became a beech, that would not be growth, but mere change. And thirdly, there is a great difference between counting apples and arriving at the mathematical formulae of modern physics. But the multiplication table is used in both and does not grow out of date.

In other words, wherever there is real progress in knowledge, there is some knowledge that is not superseded. Indeed, the very possibility of progress demands that there should be an unchanging element. New bottles for new wine, by all means: but not new palates, throats and stomachs, or it would not be, for us, 'wine' at all. I take it we should all agree to find this sort of unchanging element in the simple rules of mathematics. I would add to these the primary principles of morality. And I would also add the fundamental doctrines of Christianity. To put it in rather more technical language, I claim that the positive historical statements made by Christianity have the power, elsewhere found chiefly in formal principles, of receiving, without intrinsic change, the increasing complexity of meaning which increasing knowledge puts into them.

For example, it may be true (though I don't for a moment suppose it is) that when the Nicene Creed said 'He came down from Heaven', the writers had in mind a local movement from a local heaven to the surface of the earth – like a parachute descent. Others since may have dismissed the idea of a spatial heaven altogether. But neither the significance nor the credulity of what is asserted seems to be in the least affected by the change. On either view, the thing is miraculous: on either view, the mental images which attend the act of belief are inessential. When a Central African convert and a Harley Street specialist both affirm that Christ rose from the dead, there is, no doubt, a very great difference between their thoughts. To one, the simple picture of a dead body getting up is sufficient; the other may think of a whole series of biochemical and even physical processes beginning to work backwards. The Doctor knows that, in his experience, they never have worked backwards; but the Negro knows that dead bodies don't get up and walk. Both are faced with miracle, and both know it. If both think miracle impossible, the only difference is that the Doctor will expound the impossibility in much greater detail, will give an elaborate gloss on the simple statement that dead men don't walk about. If both believe, all the Doctor says will merely analyse and explicate the words 'He rose.' When the author of Genesis says that God made man in His own image, he may have pictured a vaguely corporeal God making man as a child makes a figure out of plasticine. A modern Christian philosopher may think of a process lasting from the first creation of matter to the final appearance on this planet of an organism fit to receive spiritual as well as biological life. But both mean essentially the same thing. Both are denying the same thing – the doctrine that matter by some blind power inherent in itself has produced spirituality.

Does this mean that Christians on different levels of general education conceal radically different beliefs under an identical form of words? Certainly not. For what they agree on is the substance, and what they differ about is the shadow. When one imagines his God seated in a local heaven above a flat earth, where another sees God and creation in terms of Professor

Whitehead's philosophy,[7] this difference touches precisely what does not matter. Perhaps this seems to you an exaggeration. But is it? As regards material reality, we are now being forced to the conclusion that we know nothing about it save its mathematics. The tangible beach and pebbles of our first calculators, the imaginable atoms of Democritus, the plain man's picture of space, turn out to be the shadow: numbers are the substance of our knowledge, the sole liaison between mind and things. What nature is in herself evades us; what seem to naïf perception to be the evident things about her, turn out to be the most phantasmal. It is something the same with our knowledge of spiritual reality. What God is in Himself, how He is to be conceived by philosophers, retreats continually from our knowledge. The elaborate world-pictures which accompany religion and which look each so solid while they last, turn out to be only shadows. It is religion itself – prayer and sacrament and repentance and adoration – which is here, in the long run, our sole avenue to the real. Like mathematics, religion can grow from within, or decay. The Jew knows more than the Pagan, the Christian more than the Jew, the modern vaguely religious man less than any of the three. But, like mathematics, it remains simply itself, capable of being applied to any new theory of the material universe and outmoded by none.

When any man comes into the presence of God he will find, whether he wishes it or not, that all those things which seemed to make him so different from the men of other times, or even from his earlier self, have fallen off him. He is back where he always was, where every man always is. *Eadem sunt omnia*

[7] Alfred North Whitehead (1861–1947).

semper.[8] Do not let us deceive ourselves. No possible complexity which we can give to our picture of the universe can hide us from God: there is no copse, no forest, no jungle thick enough to provide cover. We read in Revelation of Him that sat on the throne 'from whose face the earth and the heaven fled away'.[9] It may happen to any of us at any moment. In the twinkling of an eye, in a time too small to be measured, and in any place, all that seems to divide us from God can flee away, vanish, leaving us naked before Him, like the first man, like the only man, as if nothing but He and I existed. And since that contact cannot be avoided for long, and since it means either bliss or horror, the business of life is to learn to like it. That is the first and great commandment.

[8] Everything is always the same.
[9] Revelation 20:11.

3

Myth Became Fact
(1944)

My friend Corineus has advanced the charge that none of us are in fact Christians at all. According to him historic Christianity is something so barbarous that no modern man can really believe it: the moderns who claim to do so are in fact believing a modern system of thought which retains the vocabulary of Christianity and exploits the emotions inherited from it while quietly dropping its essential doctrines. Corineus compared modern Christianity with the modern English monarchy: the forms of kingship have been retained, but the reality has been abandoned.

All this I believe to be false, except of a few 'modernist' theologians who, by God's grace, become fewer every day. But for the moment let us assume that Corineus is right. Let us pretend, for purposes of argument, that *all* who now call themselves Christians have abandoned the historic doctrines. Let us suppose that modern 'Christianity' reveals a system of names, rituals, formulae and metaphors which persists although the thoughts behind it have changed. Corineus ought to be able to *explain* the persistence.

Why, on his view, do all these educated and enlightened pseudo-Christians insist on expressing their deepest thoughts in terms of an archaic mythology which must hamper and embarrass them at every turn? Why do they refuse to cut the umbilical cord which binds the living and flourishing child to its moribund mother? For, if Corineus is right, it should be a great relief to them to do so. Yet the odd thing is that even those who seem most embarrassed by the sediment of 'barbaric' Christianity in their thought become suddenly obstinate when you ask them to get rid of it altogether. They will strain the cord almost to breaking point, but they refuse to cut it. Sometimes they will take every step except the last one.

If all who professed Christianity were clergymen, it would be easy (though uncharitable) to reply that their livelihood depends on *not* taking that last step. Yet even if this were the true cause of their behaviour, even if all clergymen are intellectual prostitutes who preach for pay – and usually starvation pay – what they secretly believe to be false, surely so widespread a darkening of conscience among thousands of men not otherwise known to be criminal, itself demands explanation? And of course the profession of Christianity is not confined to the clergy. It is professed by millions of women and laymen who earn thereby contempt, unpopularity, suspicion, and the hostility of their own families. How does this come to happen?

Obstinacies of this sort are interesting. 'Why not cut the cord?' asks Corineus. 'Everything would be much easier if you would free your thought from this vestigial mythology.' To be sure: far easier. Life would be far easier for the mother of an invalid child if she put it into an Institution and adopted someone else's healthy baby instead. Life would be far easier to many a man if he abandoned the woman he has actually fallen in love with and married someone else because she is more suitable. The only defect of the healthy baby and the suitable woman is that they leave out the patient's only reason for bothering about a child or wife at all. 'Would not conversation be much more rational than dancing?' said Jane Austen's Miss Bingley. 'Much more rational,' replied Mr Bingley, 'but much less like a ball.'[1]

In the same way, it would be much more rational to abolish the English monarchy. But how if, by doing so, you leave out the one element in our State which matters most? How if the monarchy is the channel through which all the *vital* elements of citizenship – loyalty, the consecration of secular life, the hierarchical principle, splendour, ceremony, continuity – still trickle down to irrigate the dust-bowl of modern economic Statecraft?

The real answer of even the most 'modernist' Christianity to Corineus is the same. Even assuming (which I most constantly deny) that the doctrines of historic Christianity are merely mythical, it is the myth which is the vital and nourishing element in the whole concern. Corineus wants us to move with the times. Now, we know where times move. They move *away*. But in religion we find something that does not move away. It is what Corineus calls the myth, that abides; it is what he calls the modern and living thought that moves away. Not only the thought of theologians, but the thought of anti-theologians. Where are the predecessors of Corineus? Where is the epicureanism of Lucretius,[2] the pagan revival of Julian the Apostate?[3] Where are the Gnostics, where is the monism of Averroës,[4] the deism of

---

[1] *Pride and Prejudice*, ch. 11.
[2] Titus Lucretius Carus (c. 99–55 BC) the Roman poet.
[3] Roman emperor AD 361–3.
[4] Averroës (1126–98) of Cordova, believed that only one intellect exists for the whole human race in which every individual participates, to the exclusion of personal immortality.

Voltaire, the dogmatic materialism of the great Victorians? They have moved with the times. But the thing they were all attacking remains: Corineus finds it still there to attack. The myth (to speak his language) has outlived the thoughts of all its defenders and of all its adversaries. It is the myth that gives life. Those elements even in modernist Christianity which Corineus regards as vestigial, are the substance: what he takes for the 'real modern belief' is the shadow.

To explain this we must look a little closer at myth in general, and at this myth in particular. Human intellect is incurably abstract. Pure mathematics is the type of successful thought. Yet the only realities we experience are concrete – this pain, this pleasure, this dog, this man. While we are loving the man, bearing the pain, enjoying the pleasure, we are not intellectually apprehending Pleasure, Pain or Personality. When we begin to do so, on the other hand, the concrete realities sink to the level of mere instances or examples: we are no longer dealing with them, but with that which they exemplify. This is our dilemma – either to taste and not to know or to know and not to taste – or, more strictly, to lack one kind of knowledge because we are in an experience or to lack another kind because we are outside it. As thinkers we are cut off from what we think about; as tasting, touching, willing, loving, hating, we do not clearly understand. The more lucidly we think, the more we are cut off: the more deeply we enter into reality, the less we can think. You cannot *study* Pleasure in the moment of the nuptial embrace, nor repentance while repenting, nor analyse the nature of humour while roaring with laughter. But when else can you really know these things? 'If only my toothache would stop, I could write another chapter about Pain.' But once it stops, what do I know about pain?

Of this tragic dilemma myth is the partial solution. In the enjoyment of a great myth we come nearest to experiencing as a concrete what can otherwise be understood only as an abstraction. At this moment, for example, I am trying to understand something very abstract indeed – the fading, vanishing of tasted reality as we try to grasp it with the discursive reason. Probably I have made heavy weather of it. But if I remind you, instead, of Orpheus and Eurydice, how he was suffered to lead her by the hand but, when he turned round to look at her, she disappeared, what was merely a principle becomes imaginable. You may reply that you never till this moment attached that 'meaning' to that myth. Of course not. You are not looking for an abstract 'meaning' at all. If that was what you were doing the myth would be for you no true myth but a mere allegory. You were not knowing, but tasting; but what you were tasting turns out to be a universal principle. The moment we *state* this principle, we are admittedly back in the world of abstraction. It is only while receiving the myth as a story that you experience the principle concretely.

When we translate we get abstraction – or rather, dozens of abstractions. What flows into you from the myth is not truth but reality (truth is always *about* something, but reality is that *about which* truth is), and, therefore, every myth becomes the father of innumerable truths on the abstract level. Myth is the mountain whence all the different streams arise which become truths down here in the valley; *in hac valle abstractionis*.[5] Or, if you prefer, myth is the isthmus which connects the peninsular world of

---

[5] In this valley of separation.

thought with that vast continent we really belong to. It is not, like truth, abstract; nor is it, like direct experience, bound to the particular.

Now as myth transcends thought, Incarnation transcends myth. The heart of Christianity is a myth which is also a fact. The old myth of the Dying God, *without ceasing to be myth*, comes down from the heaven of legend and imagination to the earth of history. It *happens* – at a particular date, in a particular place, followed by definable historical consequences. We pass from a Balder or an Osiris, dying nobody knows when or where, to a historical Person crucified (it is all in order) *under Pontius Pilate*. By becoming fact it does not cease to be myth: that is the miracle. I suspect that men have sometimes derived more spiritual sustenance from myths they did not believe than from the religion they professed. To be truly Christian we must both assent to the historical fact and also receive the myth (fact though it has become) with the same imaginative embrace which we accord to all myths. The one is hardly more necessary than the other.

A man who disbelieved the Christian story as fact but continually fed on it as myth would, perhaps, be more spiritually alive than one who assented and did not think much about it. The modernist – the extreme modernist, infidel in all but name – need not be called a fool or hypocrite because he obstinately retains, even in the midst of his intellectual atheism, the language, rites, sacraments, and story of the Christians. The poor man may be clinging (with a wisdom he himself by no means understands) to that which is his life. It would have been better that Loisy[6]

---

[6] Alfred Loisy (1857–1940), a French theologian and founder of the Modernist movement.

should have remained a Christian: it would not necessarily have been better that he should have purged his thought of vestigial Christianity.

Those who do not know that this great myth became fact when the Virgin conceived are, indeed, to be pitied. But Christians also need to be reminded – we may thank Corineus for reminding us – that what became fact was a myth, that it carries with it into the world of fact all the properties of a myth. God is more than a god, not less; Christ is more than Balder, not less. We must not be ashamed of the mythical radiance resting on our theology. We must not be nervous about 'parallels' and 'Pagan Christs': they *ought* to be there – it would be a stumbling block if they weren't. We must not, in false spirituality, withhold our imaginative welcome. If God chooses to be mythopoeic – and is not the sky itself a myth? – shall we refuse to be *mythopathic*? For this is the marriage of heaven and earth: Perfect Myth and Perfect Fact: claiming not only our love and our obedience, but also our wonder and delight, addressed to the savage, the child, and the poet in each one of us no less than to the moralist, the scholar, and the philosopher.

4

Religion and Science
(1945)

'Miracles,' said my friend. 'Oh, come. Science has knocked the bottom out of all that. We know now that Nature is governed by fixed laws.'

'Didn't people always know that?' said I.

'Good Lord, no,' said he. 'For instance, take a story like the Virgin Birth. We know now that such a thing couldn't happen. We know there *must* be a male spermatozoon.'

'But look here,' said I. 'St Joseph –'

'Who's he?' asked my friend.

'He was the husband of the Virgin Mary. If you'll read the story in the Bible you'll find that when he saw his fiancée was going to have a baby he decided to cry off the marriage. Why did he do that?'

'Wouldn't most men?'

'Any man would,' said I, 'provided he knew the laws of nature – in other words, provided he knew that a girl doesn't ordinarily have a baby unless she's been sleeping with a man. But according to your theory people in the old days didn't know that nature was governed by fixed laws. I'm pointing out that the story shows that St Joseph knew *that* law just as well as you do.'

'But he came to believe in the Virgin Birth afterwards, didn't he?'

'Quite. But he didn't do so because he was under any illusion as to where babies came from in the ordinary course of nature. He believed in the Virgin Birth as something *super*-natural. He knew nature works in fixed, regular ways: but he also believed that there existed something *beyond* nature which could interfere with her workings – from outside, so to speak.'

'But modern science has shown there's no such thing.'

'Really,' said I. 'Which of the sciences?'

'Oh, well, that's a matter of detail,' said my friend. 'I can't give you chapter and verse from memory.'

'But, don't you see,' said I, 'that science never could show anything of the sort?'

'Why on earth not?'

'Because science studies nature. And the question is whether anything *besides* nature exists – anything "outside". How could you find that out by studying simply nature?'

'But don't we find out that nature *must* work in an absolutely fixed way? I mean, the laws of nature tell us not merely how things *do* happen, but how they *must* happen. No power could possibly alter them.'

'How do you mean?' said I.

'Look here,' said he. 'Could this "something outside" that you talk about make two and two five?'

'Well, no,' said I.

'All right,' said he. 'Well, I think the laws of nature are really like two and two making four. The idea of their being altered is as absurd as the idea of altering the laws of arithmetic.'

'Half a moment,' said I. 'Suppose you put sixpence into a

drawer today, and sixpence into the same drawer tomorrow. Do the laws of arithmetic make it certain you'll find a shilling's worth there the day after?'

'Of course,' said he, 'provided no one's been tampering with your drawer.'

'Ah, but that's the whole point,' said I. 'The laws of arithmetic can tell you what you'll find, with absolute certainty, *provided that* there's no interference. If a thief has been at the drawer of course you'll get a different result. But the thief won't have broken the laws of arithmetic – only the laws of England. Now, aren't the laws of nature much in the same boat? Don't they all tell you what will happen *provided* there's no interference?'

'How do you mean?'

'Well, the laws will tell you how a billiard ball will travel on a smooth surface if you hit it in a particular way – but only provided no one interferes. If, after it's already in motion, someone snatches up a cue and gives it a biff on one side – why, then, you won't get what the scientists predicted.'

'No, of course not. He can't allow for monkey-tricks like that.'

'Quite, and in the same way, if there was anything outside nature, and if it interfered – then the events which the scientist expected wouldn't follow. That would be what we call a miracle. In one sense it wouldn't break the laws of nature. The laws tell you what will happen if nothing interferes. They can't tell you whether something *is* going to interfere. I mean, it's not the expert at arithmetic who can tell you how likely someone is to interfere with the pennies in my drawer; a detective would be more use. It isn't the physicist who can tell you how likely I am to catch up a cue and spoil his experiment with the billiard ball;

you'd better ask a psychologist. And it isn't the scientist who can tell you how likely nature is to be interfered with from outside. You must go to the metaphysician.'

'These are rather niggling points,' said my friend. 'You see, the real objection goes far deeper. The whole picture of the universe which science has given us makes it such rot to believe that the Power at the back of it all could be interested in us tiny little creatures crawling about on an unimportant planet! It was all so obviously invented by people who believed in a flat earth with the stars only a mile or two away.'

'When did people believe that?'

'Why, all those old Christian chaps you're always talking about did. I mean Boethius and Augustine and Thomas Aquinas and Dante.'

'Sorry,' said I, 'but this is one of the few subjects I do know something about.'

I reached out my hand to a bookshelf. 'You see this book,' I said, 'Ptolemy's *Almagest*. You know what it is?'

'Yes,' said he. 'It's the standard astronomical handbook used all through the Middle Ages.'

'Well, just read that,' I said, pointing to Book I, chapter 5.

'The earth,' read out my friend, hesitating a bit as he translated the Latin, 'the earth, in relation to the distance of the fixed stars, has no appreciable size and must be treated as a mathematical point!'

There was another short silence.

'Did they really know that *then*?' said my friend. 'But – but none of the histories of science – none of the modern encyclopedias ever mentions the fact.'

'Exactly,' said I. 'I'll leave you to think out the reason. It almost looks as if someone was anxious to hush it up, doesn't it? I wonder why.'

There was another short silence.

'At any rate,' said I, 'we can now state the problem accurately. People usually think the problem is how to reconcile what we now know about the size of the universe with our traditional ideas of religion. That turns out not to be the problem at all. The real problem is this. The enormous size of the universe and the insignificance of the earth were known for centuries, and no one ever dreamed that they had any bearing on the religious question. Then, less than a hundred years ago, they are suddenly trotted out as an argument against Christianity. And the people who trot them out carefully hush up the fact that they were known long ago. Don't you think that all you atheists are strangely unsuspicious people?'

5

The Laws of Nature

(1945)

'Poor woman,' said my friend. 'One hardly knows what to say when they talk like that. She thinks her son survived Arnhem because she prayed for him. It would be heartless to explain to her that he really survived because he was standing a little to the left or a little to the right of some bullet. That bullet was following a course laid down by the laws of nature. It couldn't have hit him. He just happened to be standing off its line … and so all day long as regards every bullet and every splinter of shell. His survival was simply due to the laws of nature.'

At that moment my first pupil came in and the conversation was cut short, but later in the day I had to walk across the park to a committee meeting and this gave me time to think the matter over. It was quite clear that once a bullet had been fired from point A in direction B, the wind being C, and so forth, it would pursue a certain path. But might our young friend have been standing somewhere else? And might the German have fired at a different moment or in a different direction? If men have free will it would appear that they might. On that view we get a rather more complicated picture of the battle of Arnhem. The total course of events would be a kind of amalgam derived from two sources – on the one hand, from acts of human will (which might presumably have been otherwise), and, on the other, from the laws of physical nature. And this would seem to provide all that is necessary for the mother's belief that her prayers had some place among the causes of her son's preservation. God might continually influence the wills of all the combatants so as to allot death, wounds, and survival in the way He thought best, while leaving the behaviour of the projectile to follow its normal course.

But I was still not quite clear about the physical side of this picture. I had been thinking (vaguely enough) that the bullet's flight was *caused* by the laws of nature. But is this really so? Granted that the bullet is set in motion, and granted the wind and the earth's gravitation and all the other relevant factors, then it is a 'law' of nature that the bullet must take the course it did. But then the pressing of the trigger, the side wind, and even the earth, are not exactly *laws*. They are facts or events. They are not laws but things that obey laws. Obviously, to consider the pressing of the trigger would only lead us back to the free will side of the picture. We must, therefore, choose a simpler example.

The laws of physics, I understand, decree that when one billiard ball (A) sets another billiard ball (B) in motion, the momentum lost by A exactly equals the momentum gained by B. This is a *law*. That is, this is the pattern to which the movement of the two billiard balls must conform. Provided, of course, that something sets ball A in motion. And here comes the snag. The *law* won't set it in motion. It is usually a man with a cue who does that. But a man with a cue would send us back to free will, so let us assume that it was lying on a table in a liner and that what set it in motion was a lurch of the ship. In that case it was not the law which produced the movement; it was a wave. And that wave, though it certainly moved *according* to the laws of physics, was not moved by them. It was shoved by other waves, and by winds, and so forth. And however far you traced the story back you would never find the *laws* of nature causing anything.

The dazzlingly obvious conclusion now arose in my mind: *in the whole history of the universe the laws of nature have never produced a single event*. They are the pattern to which every event must conform, provided only that it can be induced to happen. But how do you get it to do that? How do you get a move on? The laws of nature can give you no help there. All events obey them, just as all operations with money obey the laws of arithmetic. Add six pennies to six and the result will certainly be a shilling. But arithmetic by itself won't put one farthing into your pocket. Up till now I had had a vague idea that the laws of nature could make things happen. I now saw that this was exactly like thinking that you could increase your income by doing sums about it. The *laws* are the pattern to which events conform: the source of events must be sought elsewhere.

This may be put in the form that the laws of nature explain everything except the source of events. But this is rather a formidable exception. The laws, in one sense, cover the whole of reality except – well, except that continuous cataract of real events which makes up the actual universe. They explain everything except what we should ordinarily call 'everything'. The only thing they omit is – the whole universe. I do not mean that a knowledge of these laws is useless. Provided we can take over the actual universe as a going concern, such knowledge is useful and indeed indispensable for manipulating it; just as, if only you have some money, arithmetic is indispensable for managing it. But the events themselves, the money itself – that is quite another affair.

Where, then, do actual events come from? In one sense the answer is easy. Each event comes from a previous event. But what happens if you trace this process backwards? To ask this is not exactly the same as to ask where *things* come from – how there came to be space and time and matter at all. Our present problem is not about things but about events; not, for example, about particles of matter but about this particle colliding with that. The mind can perhaps acquiesce in the idea that the 'properties' of the universal drama somehow 'just happen to be there': but whence comes the play, the story?

Either the stream of events had a beginning or it had not. If it had, then we are faced with something like creation. If it had not (a supposition, by the way, which some physicists find difficult), then we are faced with an everlasting impulse which, by its very nature, is opaque to scientific thought. Science, when it becomes perfect, will have explained the connection between each link in the chain and the link before it. But the actual existence of the chain will remain wholly unaccountable. We learn more and more about the pattern. We learn nothing about that which 'feeds' real events into the pattern. If it is not God, we must at the very least call it Destiny – the immaterial, ultimate, one-way pressure which keeps the universe on the move.

The smallest event, then, if we face the fact that it occurs (instead of concentrating on the pattern into which, if it can be persuaded to occur, it must fit) leads us back to a mystery which lies outside natural science. It is certainly a possible supposition that behind this mystery some mighty Will and Life is at work.

If so, any contrast between His acts and the laws of Nature is out of the question. It is His act alone that gives the laws any events to apply to. The laws are an empty frame; it is He who fills that frame – not now and then on specially 'providential' occasions, but at every moment. And He, from His vantage point above Time, can, if He pleases, take all prayers into account in ordaining that vast complex event which is the history of the universe. For what we call 'future' prayers have always been present to Him.

In *Hamlet* a branch breaks and Ophelia is drowned. Did she die because the branch broke or because Shakespeare wanted her to die at that point in the play? Either – both – whichever you please. The alternative suggested by the question is not a real alternative at all – once you have grasped that Shakespeare is making the whole play.

6

The Grand Miracle
(1945)

One is very often asked at present whether we could not have a Christianity stripped, or, as people who ask it say, 'freed' from its miraculous elements, a Christianity with the miraculous elements suppressed. Now, it seems to me that precisely the one religion in the world, or, at least, the only one I know, with which you could not do that is Christianity. In a religion like Buddhism, if you took away the miracles attributed to Gautama Buddha in some very late sources, there would be no loss; in fact, the religion would get on very much better without them because in that case the miracles largely contradict the teaching. Or even in the case of a religion like Mohammedanism, nothing essential would be altered if you took away the miracles. You could have a great prophet preaching his dogmas without bringing in any miracles; they are only in the nature of a digression, or illuminated capitals. But you cannot possibly do that with Christianity, because the Christian story is precisely the story of one grand miracle, the Christian assertion being that what is beyond all space and time, what is uncreated, eternal, came into nature, into human nature, descended into His own universe, and rose again, bringing nature up with Him. It is precisely one great miracle. If you take that away there is nothing specifically Christian left. There may be many admirable human things which Christianity shares with all other systems in the world, but there would be nothing specifically Christian. Conversely, once you have accepted that, then you will see that all other well-established Christian miracles – because, of course, there are ill-established Christian miracles; there are Christian legends just as much as there are heathen legends, or modern journalistic legends – you will see that all the well-established Christian miracles are part of it, that they all either prepare for, or exhibit, or result from the Incarnation. Just as every natural event exhibits the total character of the natural universe at a particular point and space of time; so every miracle exhibits the character of the Incarnation.

Now, if one asks whether that central grand miracle in Christianity is itself probable or improbable, of course, quite clearly you cannot be applying Hume's[1] kind of probability. You cannot mean a probability based on statistics according to which the more often a thing has happened, the more likely it is to happen again (the more often you get indigestion from eating a certain food, the more probable it is, if you eat it again, that you will again have indigestion). Certainly the Incarnation cannot be probable in that sense. It is of its very nature to have happened only once. But then it is of the very nature of the history of this world to have happened only once; and if the Incarnation happened at all, it is the central chapter of that history. It is improbable in the same way in which the whole of nature is improbable,

[1] David Hume (1711–76), Scottish philosopher and historian. See especially the 'Essay upon Miracles' in his *Philosophical Essays Concerning Human Understanding* (1748).

because it is only there once, and will happen only once. So one must apply to it a quite different kind of standard.

I think we are rather in this position. Supposing you had before you a manuscript of some great work, either a symphony or a novel. There then comes to you a person, saying, 'Here is a new bit of the manuscript that I found; it is the central passage of that symphony, or the central chapter of that novel. The text is incomplete without it. I have got the missing passage which is really the centre of the whole work.' The only thing you could do would be to put this new piece of the manuscript in that central position, and then see how it reacted on the whole of the rest of the work. If it constantly brought out new meanings for the whole of the rest of the work, if it made you notice things in the rest of the work which you had not noticed before, then I think you would decide that it was authentic. On the other hand, if it failed to do that, then, however attractive it was in itself, you would reject it.

Now, what is the missing chapter in this case, the chapter which Christians are offering? The story of the Incarnation is the story of a descent and resurrection. When I say 'resurrection' here, I am not referring simply to the first few hours, or the first few weeks of the Resurrection. I am talking of this whole, huge pattern of descent, down, down, and then up again. What we ordinarily call the Resurrection being just, so to speak, the point at which it turns. Think what that descent is. The coming down, not only into humanity, but into those nine months which precede human birth, in which they tell us we all recapitulate strange pre-human, sub-human forms of life, and going lower still into being a corpse, a thing which, if this ascending movement had not begun, would presently have passed out of the organic altogether, and have gone back into the inorganic, as all corpses do. One has a picture of someone going right down and dredging the sea-bottom. One has a picture of a strong man trying to lift a very big, complicated burden. He stoops down and gets himself right under it so that he himself disappears; and then he straightens his back and moves off with the whole thing swaying on his shoulders. Or else one has the picture of a diver, stripping off garment after garment, making himself naked, then flashing for a moment in the air, and then down through the green, and warm, and sunlit water into the pitch black, cold, freezing water, down into the mud and slime, then up again, his lungs almost bursting, back again to the green and warm and sunlit water, and then at last out into the sunshine, holding in his hand the dripping thing he went down to get. This thing is human nature; but, associated with it, all nature, the new universe. That indeed is a point I cannot go into tonight, because it would take a whole sermon – this connection between human nature and nature in general. It sounds startling, but I believe it can be fully justified.

Now, as soon as you have thought of this, this pattern of the huge dive down to the bottom, into the depths of the universe and coming up again into the light, everyone will see at once how that is imitated and echoed by the principles of the natural world; the descent of the seed into the soil, and its rising again in the plants. There are also all sorts of things in our own spiritual life where a thing has to be killed, and broken, in order that it may then become bright, and strong, and splendid. The analogy is obvious. In that sense the doctrine fits in very well, so well in fact that immediately there comes the suspicion. Is it not fitting in a great deal too well? In other words, does not the Christian story show this pattern of descent and re-ascent because that is part of all the nature religions of the world? We have read about it in *The Golden Bough*.[2] We all know about Adonis, and the stories of the rest of those rather tedious people; is not this one more instance of the same thing, 'the dying God'? Well, yes it is. That is what makes the question subtle. What the anthropological critic of Christianity is always saying is perfectly true. Christ *is* a figure of that sort. And here comes a very curious thing. When I first, after childhood, read the Gospels, I was full of that stuff about the dying God, *The Golden Bough*, and so on. It was to me then a very poetic, and mysterious, and quickening idea; and when I turned to the Gospels never will I forget my disappointment and repulsion at finding hardly anything about it at all. The metaphor of the seed dropping into the ground in this connection occurs (I think) twice in the New Testament,[3] and for the rest hardly any notice is taken; it seemed to me extraordinary. You had a dying God, Who was always representative of the corn: you see Him holding the corn, that is, bread, in His hand, and saying, 'This is My Body,'[4] and from my point of view, as I then was, He did not seem to realize what He was saying. Surely there, if anywhere, this connection between the Christian story and the corn must have come out; the whole context is crying out for it. But everything goes on as if the principal actor and still more those about Him, were totally ignorant of what they were doing. It is as if you got very good evidence concerning the sea-serpent, but the men who brought this good evidence seemed never to have heard of sea-serpents. Or to put it in

[2] By Sir James George Frazer (1890).
[3] John 12:24; 1 Corinthians 15:36.
[4] Matthew 26:26; Mark 14:22; Luke 22:19; 1 Corinthians 11:24.

another way, why was it that the only case of the 'dying God' which might conceivably have been historical occurred among a people (and the only people in the whole Mediterranean world) who had not got any trace of this nature religion, and indeed seem to know nothing about it? Why is it among *them* the thing suddenly appears to happen?

The principal actor, humanly speaking, hardly seems to know of the repercussions His words (and sufferings) would have in any pagan mind. Well, that is almost explicable, except on one hypothesis. How if the corn king is not mentioned in that Book, because He is here of whom the corn king was an image? How if the representation is absent because here at last, the thing represented is present? If the shadows are absent because the thing of which they were shadows is here? The corn itself is in its far-off way an imitation of the supernatural reality; the thing dying, and coming to life again, descending, and re-ascending beyond all nature. The principle is there in nature because it was first there in God Himself. Thus one is getting in behind the nature religions, and behind nature to Someone Who is not explained by, but explains, not indeed, the nature religions directly, but that whole characteristic behaviour of nature on which nature religions were based. Well, that is one way in which it surprised me. It seemed to fit in in a very peculiar way, showing me something about nature more fully than I had seen it before, while itself remaining quite outside and above the nature religions.

Then another thing. We, with our modern democratic and arithmetical presuppositions would so have liked and expected all men to start equal in their search for God. One has the picture of great centripetal roads coming from all directions, with well-disposed people, all meaning the same thing, and getting closer and closer together. How shockingly opposite to that is the Christian story! One people picked out of the whole earth; that people purged and proved again and again. Some are lost in the desert before they reach Palestine; some stay in Babylon; some becoming indifferent. The whole thing narrows and narrows, until at last it comes down to a little point, small as the point of a spear – a Jewish girl at her prayers. That is what the whole of human nature has narrowed down to before the Incarnation takes place. Very unlike what we expected, but, of course, not in the least unlike what seems, in general, as shown by nature, to be God's way of working. The universe is quite a shockingly selective, undemocratic place out of apparently infinite space, a relatively tiny proportion occupied by matter of any kind. Of the stars perhaps only one has planets: of the planets only one is at all likely to sustain organic life. Of the animals only one species is rational. Selection as seen in nature, and the appalling waste which it involves, appears a horrible and an unjust thing by human standards. But the selectiveness in the Christian story is not quite like that. The people who are selected are, in a sense, unfairly selected for a supreme honour; but it is also a supreme burden. The People of Israel come to realize that it is their woes which are saving the world. Even in human society, though, one sees how this inequality furnishes an opportunity for every kind of tyranny and servility. Yet, on the other hand, one also sees that it furnishes an opportunity for some of the very best things we can think of – humility, and kindness, and the immense pleasures of admiration. (I cannot conceive how one would get through the boredom of a world in which you never met anyone more clever, or more beautiful, or stronger than yourself. The very crowds who go after the football celebrities and film stars know better than to desire that kind of equality!) What the story of the Incarnation seems to be doing is to flash a new light on a principle in nature, and to show for the first time that this principle of inequality in nature is neither good nor bad. It is a common theme running through both the goodness and badness of the natural world, and I begin to see how it can survive as a supreme beauty in a redeemed universe.

And with that I have unconsciously passed over to the third point. I have said that the selectiveness was not unfair in the way in which we first suspect, because those selected for the great honour are also selected for the great suffering, and their suffering heals others. In the Incarnation we get, of course, this idea of vicariousness of one person profiting by the earnings of another person. In its highest form that is the very centre of Christianity. And we also find this same vicariousness to be a characteristic, or, as the musician would put it, a *leit-motif* of nature. It is a law of the natural universe that no being can exist on its own resources. Everyone, everything, is hopelessly indebted to everyone and everything else. In the universe, as we now see it, this is the source of many of the greatest horrors: all the horrors of carnivorousness, and the worse horrors of the parasites, those horrible animals that live under the skin of other animals, and so on. And yet, suddenly seeing it in the light of the Christian story, one realizes that vicariousness is not in itself bad; that all these animals and insects and horrors are merely that principle of vicariousness twisted in one way. For when you think it out, nearly everything good in nature also comes from vicariousness. After all, the child, both before and after birth, lives on its mother, just as the parasite lives on its host, the one being a horror, the other being the source of almost every natural goodness in the world.

It all depends upon what you do with this principle. So that I find in that third way also, that what is implied by the Incarnation just fits in exactly with what I have seen in nature, and (this is the important point) each time it gives it a new twist. If I accept this supposed missing chapter, the Incarnation, I find it begins to illuminate the whole of the rest of the manuscript. It lights up nature's pattern of death and rebirth; and, secondly, her selectiveness; and, thirdly, her vicariousness.

Now I notice a very odd point. All other religions in the world, as far as I know them, are either nature religions, or anti-nature religions. The nature religions are those of the old, simple pagan sort that you know about. You actually got drunk in the temple of Bacchus. You actually committed fornication in the temple of Aphrodite. The more modern form of nature religion would be the religion started, in a sense, by Bergson[5] (but he repented, and died Christian), and carried on in a more popular form by Mr Bernard Shaw. The anti-nature religions are those like Hinduism and Stoicism, where men say, 'I will starve my flesh. I care not whether I live or die.' All natural things are to be set aside: the aim is Nirvana, apathy, negative spirituality. The nature religions simply affirm my natural desires. The anti-natural religions simply contradict them. The nature religions simply give a new sanction to what I already always thought about the universe in my moments of rude health and cheerful brutality. The anti-nature religions merely repeat what I always thought about it in my moods of lassitude, or delicacy, or compassion.

---

[5] Henri Bergson (1859–1941). His 'nature religion' is particularly evident in his *Matière et Mémoire* (1896) and *L'Evolution Créatrice* (1907).

But here is something quite different. Here is something telling me – well, what? Telling me that I must never, like the Stoics, say that death does not matter. Nothing is less Christian than that. Death which made Life Himself shed tears at the grave of Lazarus,[6] and shed tears of blood in Gethsemane.[7] This is an appalling horror; a stinking indignity. (You remember Thomas Browne's splendid remark: 'I am not so much afraid of death, as ashamed of it.')[8] And yet, somehow or other, infinitely good. Christianity does not simply affirm or simply deny the horror of death: it tells me something quite new about it. Again it does not, like Nietzsche, simply confirm my desire to be stronger, or cleverer than other people. On the other hand, it does not allow me to say, 'Oh, Lord, won't there be a day when everyone will be as good as everyone else?' In the same way, about vicariousness. It will not, in any way, allow me to be an exploiter, to act as a parasite on other people; yet it will not allow me any dream of living on my own. It will teach me to accept with glad humility the enormous sacrifice that others make for me, as well as to make sacrifices for others.

That is why I think this Grand Miracle is the missing chapter in this novel, the chapter on which the whole plot turns; that is why I believe that God really has dived down into the bottom of creation, and has come up bringing the whole redeemed nature on His shoulders. The miracles that have already happened are, of course, as Scripture so often says, the first fruits of that cosmic

[6] John 11:35.
[7] Luke 22:44.
[8] 'I am not so much afraid of death, as ashamed thereof.' *Religio Medici*, First Part, Section 40.

summer which is presently coming on.[9] Christ has risen, and so we shall rise. St Peter for a few seconds walked on the water;[10] and the day will come when there will be a re-made universe, infinitely obedient to the will of glorified and obedient men, when we can do all things, when we shall be those gods that we are described as being in Scripture. To be sure, it feels wintry enough still: but often in the very early spring it feels like that. Two thousand years are only a day or two by this scale. A man really ought to say, 'The Resurrection happened two thousand years ago' in the same spirit in which he says, 'I saw a crocus yesterday.' Because we know what is coming behind the crocus. The spring comes slowly down this way; but the great thing is that the corner has been turned. There is, of course, this difference, that in the natural spring the crocus cannot choose whether it will respond or not. We can. We have the power either of withstanding the spring, and sinking back into the cosmic winter, or of going on into those 'high mid-summer pomps' in which our Leader, the Son of Man, already dwells, and to which He is calling us. It remains with us to follow or not, to die in this winter, or to go on into that spring and that summer.

---

[9] Romans 8:23; 11:16; 16:5; 1 Corinthians 15:20; James 1:18; Revelation 14:4.
[10] Matthew 14:29.

7

Man or Rabbit?
(1946)

'Can't you lead a good life without believing in Christianity?'
This is the question on which I have been asked to write, and
straightaway, before I begin trying to answer it, I have a com-
ment to make. The question sounds as if it were asked by a person who said to himself, 'I don't care whether Christianity is in
fact true or not. I'm not interested in finding out whether the
real universe is more like what the Christians say than what the
Materialists say. All I'm interested in is leading a good life.
I'm going to choose beliefs not because I think them true but
because I find them helpful.' Now frankly, I find it hard to sym-
pathize with this state of mind. One of the things that distin-
guishes man from the other animals is that he wants to know
things, wants to find out what reality is like, simply for the sake
of knowing. When that desire is completely quenched in anyone, I think he has become something less than human. As a
matter of fact, I don't believe any of you have really lost that
desire. More probably, foolish preachers, by always telling you
how much Christianity will help you and how good it is for
society, have actually led you to forget that Christianity is not a
patent medicine. Christianity claims to give an account of *facts* –

to tell you what the real universe is like. Its account of the universe may be true, or it may not, and once the question is really before you, then your natural inquisitiveness must make you want to know the answer. If Christianity is untrue, then no honest man will want to believe it, however helpful it might be: if it is true, every honest man will want to believe it, even if it gives him no help at all.

As soon as we have realized this, we realize something else. If Christianity should happen to be true, then it is quite impossible that those who know this truth and those who don't should be equally well equipped for leading a good life. Knowledge of the facts must make a difference to one's actions. Suppose you found a man on the point of starvation and wanted to do the right thing. If you had no knowledge of medical science, you would probably give him a large solid meal; and as a result your man would die. That is what comes of working in the dark. In the same way a Christian and a non-Christian may both wish to do good to their fellow men. The one believes that men are going to live for ever, that they were created by God and so built that they can find their true and lasting happiness only by being united to God, that they have gone badly off the rails, and that obedient faith in Christ is the only way back. The other believes that men are an accidental result of the blind workings of matter, that they started as mere animals and have more or less steadily improved, that they are going to live for about seventy years, that their happiness is fully attainable by good social services and political organizations, and that everything else (e.g. vivisection, birth-control, the judicial system, education) is to be judged to be 'good' or 'bad' simply in so far as it helps or hinders that kind of 'happiness'.

Now there are quite a lot of things which these two men could agree in doing for their fellow citizens. Both would approve of efficient sewers and hospitals and a healthy diet. But sooner or later the difference of their beliefs would produce differences in their practical proposals. Both, for example, might be very keen about education: but the kinds of education they wanted people to have would obviously be very different. Again, where the Materialist would simply ask about a proposed action 'Will it increase the happiness of the majority?', the Christian might have to say, 'Even if it does increase the happiness of the majority, we can't do it. It is unjust.' And all the time, one great difference would run through their whole policy. To the Materialist things like nations, classes, civilizations must be more important than individuals, because the individuals live only seventy odd years each and the group may last for centuries. But to the Christian, individuals are more important, for they live eternally; and races, civilizations and the like, are in comparison the creatures of a day.

The Christian and the Materialist hold different beliefs about the universe. They can't both be right. The one who is wrong will act in a way which simply doesn't fit the real universe. Consequently, with the best will in the world, he will be helping his fellow creatures to their destruction.

With the best will in the world ... then it won't be his fault? Surely God (if there is a God) will not punish a man for honest mistakes? But was *that* all you were thinking about? Are we ready to run the risk of working in the dark all our lives and doing infinite harm, provided only someone will assure us that our own skins will be safe, that no one will punish us or blame us? I will not believe that the reader is quite on that level. But even if he were, there is something to be said to him.

The question before each of us is not 'Can *someone* lead a good life without Christianity?' The question is, 'Can *I*?' We all know there have been good men who were not Christians; men like Socrates and Confucius who had never heard of it, or men like J. S. Mill who quite honestly couldn't believe it. Supposing Christianity to be true, these men were in a state of honest ignorance or honest error. If their intentions were as good as I suppose them to have been (for of course I can't read their secret hearts) I hope and believe that the skill and mercy of God will remedy the evils which their ignorance, left to itself, would naturally produce both for them and for those whom they influenced. But the man who asks me, 'Can't I lead a good life without believing in Christianity?' is clearly not in the same position. If he hadn't heard of Christianity he would not be asking this question. If, having heard of it, and having seriously considered it, he had decided that it was untrue, then once more he would not be asking the question. The man who asks this question has heard of Christianity and is by no means certain that it may not be true. He is really asking, 'Need I bother about it? Mayn't I just evade the issue, just let sleeping dogs lie, and get on with being "good"? Aren't good intentions enough to keep me safe and blameless without knocking at that dreadful door and making sure whether there is, or isn't, someone inside?'

To such a man it might be enough to reply that he is really asking to be allowed to get on with being 'good' before he has done his best to discover what *good* means. But that is not the whole story. We need not enquire whether God will punish him for his cowardice and laziness; they will punish themselves. The man is shirking. He is deliberately trying not to know whether

Christianity is true or false, because he foresees endless trouble if it should turn out to be true. He is like the man who deliberately 'forgets' to look at the notice board because, if he did, he might find his name down for some unpleasant duty. He is like the man who won't look at his bank account because he's afraid of what he might find there. He is like the man who won't go to the doctor when he first feels a mysterious pain, because he is afraid of what the doctor may tell him.

The man who remains an unbeliever for such reasons is not in a state of honest error. He is in a state of dishonest error, and that dishonesty will spread through all his thoughts and actions: a certain shiftiness, a vague worry in the background, a blunting of his whole mental edge, will result. He has lost his intellectual virginity. Honest rejection of Christ, however mistaken, will be forgiven and healed – 'Whosoever shall speak a word against the Son of Man, it shall be forgiven him.'[1] But to *evade* the Son of Man, to look the other way, to pretend you haven't noticed, to become suddenly absorbed in something on the other side of the street, to leave the receiver off the telephone because it might be He who was ringing up, to leave unopened certain letters in a strange handwriting because they might be from Him – this is a different matter. You may not be certain yet whether you ought to be a Christian; but you do know you ought to be a man, not an ostrich, hiding its head in the sands.

But still – for intellectual honour has sunk very low in our age – I hear someone whimpering on with his question, 'Will it help me? Will it make me happy? Do you really think I'd be better if I became a Christian?' Well, if you must have it, my answer is

---

[1] Luke 12:10.

'Yes'. But I don't like giving an answer at all at this stage. Here is a door, behind which, according to some people, the secret of the universe is waiting for you. Either that's true, or it isn't. And if it isn't, then what the door really conceals is simply the greatest fraud, the most colossal 'sell' on record. Isn't it obviously the job of every man (that is a man and not a rabbit) to try to find out which, and then to devote his full energies either to serving this tremendous secret or to exposing and destroying this gigantic humbug? Faced with such an issue, can you really remain wholly absorbed in your blessed 'moral development'?

All right, Christianity will do you good – a great deal more good than you ever wanted or expected. And the first bit of good it will do you is to hammer into your head (you won't enjoy *that*!) the fact that what you have hitherto called 'good' – all that about 'leading a decent life' and 'being kind' – isn't quite the magnificent and all-important affair you supposed. It will teach you that in fact you can't be 'good' (not for twenty-four hours) on your own moral efforts. And then it will teach you that even if you were, you still wouldn't have achieved the purpose for which you were created. Mere *morality* is not the end of life. You were made for something quite different from that. J. S. Mill and Confucius (Socrates was much nearer the reality) simply didn't know what life is about. The people who keep on asking if they can't lead a decent life without Christ, don't know what life is about; if they did they would know that 'a decent life' is mere machinery compared with the thing we men are really made for. Morality is indispensable: but the Divine Life, which gives itself to us and which calls us to be gods, intends for us something in which morality will be swallowed up. We are to be re-made. All the rabbit in us is to disappear – the worried, conscientious, ethical rabbit as well as the cowardly and sensual rabbit. We shall bleed and squeal as the handfuls of fur come out; and then, surprisingly, we shall find underneath it all a thing we have never yet imagined: a real man, an ageless god, a son of God, strong, radiant, wise, beautiful, and drenched in joy.

'When that which is perfect is come, then that which is in part shall be done away.'[2] The idea of reaching 'a good life' without Christ is based on a double error. Firstly, we cannot do it; and secondly, in setting up 'a good life' as our final goal, we have missed the very point of our existence. Morality is a mountain which we cannot climb by our own efforts; and if we could we should only perish in the ice and unbreathable air of the summit, lacking those wings with which the rest of the journey has to be accomplished. For it is *from* there that the real ascent begins. The ropes and axes are 'done away' and the rest is a matter of flying.

[2] 1 Corinthians 13:10.

8

'The Trouble With "X" ...'
(1948)

I suppose I may assume that seven out of ten of those who read these lines are in some kind of difficulty about some other human being. Either at work or at home, either the people who employ you or those whom you employ, either those who share your house or those whose house you share, either your in-laws or parents or children, your wife or your husband, are making life harder for you than it need be even in these days. It is to be hoped that we do not often mention these difficulties (especially the domestic ones) to outsiders. But sometimes we do. An outside friend asks us why we are looking so glum; and the truth comes out.

On such occasions the outside friend usually says, 'But why don't you tell them? Why don't you go to your wife (or husband, or father, or daughter, or boss, or landlady, or lodger) and have it all out? People are usually reasonable. All you've got to do is to make them see things in the right light. Explain it to them in a reasonable, quiet, friendly way.' And we, whatever we say outwardly, think sadly to ourselves, 'He doesn't know "X".' We do. We know how utterly hopeless it is to make 'X' see reason. Either we've tried it over and over again – tried it till we are sick of trying it – or else we've never tried it because we saw from the beginning how useless it would be. We know that if we attempt to 'have it all out with "X"'there will either be a 'scene', or else 'X' will stare at us in blank amazement and say 'I don't know what on earth you're talking about'; or else (which is perhaps worst of all) 'X' will quite agree with us and promise to turn over a new leaf and put everything on a new footing – and then, twenty-four hours later, will be exactly the same as 'X' has always been.

You know, in fact, that any attempt to talk things over with 'X' will shipwreck on the old, fatal flaw in 'X's' character. And you see, looking back, how all the plans you have ever made always have shipwrecked on that fatal flaw – on 'X's' incurable jealousy, or laziness, or touchiness, or muddle-headedness, or bossiness, or ill temper, or changeableness. Up to a certain age you have perhaps had the illusion that some external stroke of good fortune – an improvement in health, a rise of salary, the end of the war – would solve your difficulty. But you know better now. The war is over, and you realize that even if the other things happened, 'X' would still be 'X', and you would still be up against the same old problem. Even if you became a millionaire, your husband would still be a bully, or your wife would still nag or your son would still drink, or you'd still have to have your mother-in-law to live with you.

It is a great step forward to realize that this is so; to face the fact that even if all external things went right, real happiness would still depend on the character of the people you have to live with – and that you can't alter their characters. And now comes the point. When you have seen this you have, for the first time, had a glimpse of what it must be like for God. For, of course, this is (in one way) just what God Himself is up against. He has provided a rich, beautiful world for people to live in. He has given them intelligence to show them how it can be used, and conscience to show them how it ought to be used. He has contrived that the things they need for their biological life (food, drink, rest, sleep, exercise) should be positively delightful to them. And, having done all this, He then sees all His plans spoiled – just as our little plans are spoiled – by the crookedness of the people themselves. All the things He has given them to be happy with they turn into occasions for quarrelling and jealousy, and excess and hoarding, and tomfoolery.

You may say it is very different for God because He could, if He pleased, alter people's characters, and we can't. But this difference doesn't go quite as deep as we may at first think. God has made it a rule for Himself that He won't alter people's character by force. He can and will alter them – but only if the people will let Him. In that way He has really and truly limited His power. Sometimes we wonder why He has done so, or even wish that He hadn't. But apparently He thinks it worth doing. He would rather have a world of free beings, with all its risks, than a world of people who did right like machines because they couldn't do anything else. The more we succeed in imagining what a world of perfect automatic beings would be like, the more, I think, we shall see His wisdom.

I said that when we see how all our plans shipwreck on the characters of the people we have to deal with, we are 'in *one* way' seeing what it must be like for God. But only in one way. There are two respects in which God's view must be very different from ours. In the first place, He sees (like you) how all the people in your home or your job are in various degrees awkward or difficult; but when He looks into that home or factory or office He sees one more person of the same kind – the one you never do see. I mean, of course, yourself. That is the next great step in wisdom – to realize that you also are just that sort of person. You also have a fatal flaw in your character. All the hopes and plans of others have again and again shipwrecked on your character just as your hopes and plans have shipwrecked on theirs.

It is no good passing this over with some vague, general admission such as 'Of course, I know I have my faults.' It is important to realize that there is some really fatal flaw in you: something which gives the others just that same feeling of *despair* which their flaws give you. And it is almost certainly something you don't know about – like what the advertisements call 'halitosis', which everyone notices except the person who has it. But why, you ask, don't the others tell me? Believe me, they have tried to tell you over and over again, and you just couldn't 'take it'. Perhaps a good deal of what you call their 'nagging' or 'bad temper' or 'queerness' are just their attempts to make you see the truth. And even the faults you do know you don't know fully. You say, 'I admit I lost my temper last night'; but the others know that you're always doing it, that you are a bad-tempered person. You say, 'I admit I drank too much last Saturday'; but everyone else knows that you are a habitual drunkard.

That is one way in which God's view must differ from mine. He sees all the characters: I see all except my own. But the second difference is this. He loves the people in spite of their faults. He goes on loving. He does not let go. Don't say, 'It's all very well for Him; He hasn't got to live with them.' He has. He is inside them as well as outside them. He is *with* them far more intimately and closely and incessantly than we can ever be. Every vile thought within their minds (and ours), every moment of spite, envy, arrogance, greed and self-conceit comes right up against His patient and longing love, and grieves His spirit more than it grieves ours.

The more we can imitate God in both these respects, the more progress we shall make. We must love 'X' more; and we must learn to see ourselves as a person of exactly the same kind. Some people say it is morbid to be always thinking of one's own faults. That would be all very well if most of us could stop thinking of our own without soon beginning to think about those of other people. For unfortunately we *enjoy* thinking about other people's faults: and in the proper sense of the word 'morbid', that is the most morbid pleasure in the world.

We don't like rationing which is imposed upon us, but I suggest one form of rationing which we ought to impose on ourselves. Abstain from all thinking about other people's faults, unless your duties as a teacher or parent make it necessary to think about them. Whenever the thoughts come unnecessarily into one's mind, why not simply shove them away? And think of one's own faults instead? For there, with God's help, one *can* do something. Of all the awkward people in your house or job there is only one whom you can improve very much. That is the practical end at which to begin. And really, we'd better. The job has to be tackled some day: and every day we put it off will make it harder to begin.

What, after all, is the alternative? You see clearly enough that nothing, not even God with all His power, can make 'X' really happy as long as 'X' remains envious, self-centred, and spiteful. Be sure there is something inside you which, unless it is altered, will put it out of God's power to prevent your being eternally miserable. While that something remains there can be no Heaven for you, just as there can be no sweet smells for a man with a cold in the nose, and no music for a man who is deaf. It's not a question of God 'sending' us to Hell. In each of us there is something growing up which will of itself *be Hell* unless it is nipped in the bud. The matter is serious: let us put ourselves in His hands at once – this very day, this hour.

9

What Are We to Make of Jesus Christ?
(1950)

'What are we to make of Jesus Christ?' This is a question which has, in a sense, a frantically comic side. For the real question is not what are we to make of Christ, but what is He to make of us? The picture of a fly sitting deciding what it is going to make of an elephant has comic elements about it. But perhaps the questioner meant what are we to make of Him in the sense of 'How are we to solve the historical problem set us by the recorded sayings and acts of this Man?' This problem is to reconcile two things. On the one hand you have got the almost generally admitted depth and sanity of His moral teaching, which is not very seriously questioned, even by those who are opposed to Christianity. In fact, I find when I am arguing with very anti-God people that they rather make a point of saying, 'I am entirely in favour of the moral teaching of Christianity' – and there seems to be a general agreement that in the teaching of this Man and of His immediate followers, moral truth is exhibited at its purest and best. It is not sloppy idealism, it is full of wisdom and shrewdness. The whole thing is realistic, fresh to the highest degree, the product of a sane mind. That is one phenomenon.

The other phenomenon is the quite appalling nature of this Man's theological remarks. You all know what I mean, and I want rather to stress the point that the appalling claim which this Man seems to be making is not merely made at one moment of His career. There is, of course, the one moment which led to His execution. The moment at which the High Priest said to Him, 'Who are you?' 'I am the Anointed, the Son of the uncreated God, and you shall see Me appearing at the end of all history as the judge of the universe.' But that claim, in fact, does not rest on this one dramatic moment. When you look into His conversation you will find this sort of claim running throughout the whole thing. For instance, He went about saying to people, 'I forgive your sins.' Now it is quite natural for a man to forgive something you do to *him*. Thus if somebody cheats *me* out of five pounds it is quite possible and reasonable for me to say, 'Well, I forgive him, we will say no more about it.' What on earth would you say if somebody had done *you* out of five pounds and *I* said, 'That is all right, I forgive him'? Then there is a curious thing which seems to slip out almost by accident. On one occasion this Man is sitting looking down on Jerusalem from the hill above it and suddenly in comes an extraordinary remark – 'I keep on sending you prophets and wise men.' Nobody comments on it. And yet, quite suddenly, almost incidentally, He is claiming to be the power that all through the centuries is sending wise men and leaders into the world. Here is another curious remark: in almost every religion there are unpleasant observances like fasting. This Man suddenly remarks one day, 'No one need fast while I am here.' Who is this Man who remarks that His mere presence suspends all normal rules? Who is the person who can suddenly tell the School they can have a half-holiday? Sometimes the statements put forward the assumption that He, the Speaker, is completely without sin or fault. This is always the attitude. 'You, to whom I am talking, are all sinners,' and He never remotely suggests that this same reproach can be brought against Him. He says again, 'I am the begotten of the One God; before Abraham was, I am,' and remember what the words 'I am' were in Hebrew. They were the name of God, which must not be spoken by any human being, the name which it was death to utter.

Well, that is the other side. On the one side clear, definite moral teaching. On the other, claims which, if not true, are those of a megalomaniac, compared with whom Hitler was the most sane and humble of men. There is no half-way house and there is no parallel in other religions. If you had gone to Buddha and asked him: 'Are you the son of Bramah?' he would have said, 'My son, you are still in the vale of illusion.' If you had gone to Socrates and asked, 'Are you Zeus?' he would have laughed at you. If you had gone to Mohammed and asked, 'Are you Allah?' he would first have rent his clothes and then cut your head off. If you had asked Confucius, 'Are you Heaven?', I think he would have probably replied, 'Remarks which are not in accordance with nature are in bad taste.' The idea of a great moral teacher saying what Christ said is out of the question. In my opinion, the only person who can say that sort of thing is either God or a complete lunatic suffering from that form of delusion which undermines the whole mind of man. If you think you are a poached egg, when you are looking for a piece of toast to suit you, you may be sane, but if you think you are God, there is no chance for you. We may note in passing that He was never regarded as a mere moral teacher. He did not produce that effect on any of the people who actually met him. He produced mainly three effects – Hatred – Terror – Adoration. There was no trace of people expressing mild approval.

What are we to do about reconciling the two contradictory phenomena? One attempt consists in saying that the Man did not really say these things, but that His followers exaggerated the story, and so the legend grew up that He had said them. This is difficult because His followers were all Jews; that is, they belonged to that Nation which of all others was most convinced that there was only one God – that there could not possibly be another. It is very odd that this horrible invention about a religious leader should grow up among the one people in the whole earth least likely to make such a mistake. On the contrary we get the impression that none of His immediate followers or even of the New Testament writers embraced the doctrine at all easily.

Another point is that on that view you would have to regard the accounts of the Man as being *legends*. Now, as a literary historian, I am perfectly convinced that whatever else the Gospels are they are not legends. I have read a great deal of legend and I am quite clear that they are not the same sort of thing. They are not artistic enough to be legends. From an imaginative point of view they are clumsy, they don't work up to things properly. Most of the life of Jesus is totally unknown to us, as is the life of anyone else who lived at that time, and no people building up a legend would allow that to be so. Apart from bits of the Platonic dialogues, there are no conversations that I know of in ancient literature like the Fourth Gospel. There is nothing, even in modern literature, until about a hundred years ago when the realistic novel came into existence. In the story of the woman taken in adultery we are told Christ bent down and scribbled in the dust with His finger. Nothing comes of this. No one has ever based any doctrine on it. And the art of *inventing* little irrelevant details to make an imaginary scene more convincing is a purely modern art. Surely the only explanation of this passage is that the thing really happened? The author put it in simply because he had *seen* it.

Then we come to the strangest story of all, the story of the Resurrection. It is very necessary to get the story clear. I heard a man say, 'The importance of the Resurrection is that it gives evidence of survival, evidence that the human personality survives death.' On that view what happened to Christ would be what had always happened to all men, the difference being that in Christ's case we were privileged to see it happening. This is certainly not what the earliest Christian writers thought. Something perfectly new in the history of the universe had happened. Christ had defeated death. The door which had always been locked had for the very first time been forced open. This is something quite distinct from mere ghost-survival. I don't mean that they disbelieved in ghost-survival. On the contrary, they believed in it so firmly that, on more than one occasion, Christ had had to assure them that He was *not* a ghost. The point is that while believing in survival they yet regarded the Resurrection as something totally different and new. The Resurrection narratives are not a picture of survival after death; they record how a totally new mode of being has arisen in the universe. Something new has appeared in the universe: as new as the first coming of organic life. This Man, after death, does not get divided into 'ghost' and 'corpse'. A new mode of being has arisen. That is the story. What are we going to make of it?

The question is, I suppose, whether any hypothesis covers the facts so well as the Christian hypothesis. That hypothesis is that God has come down into the created universe, down to manhood – and come up again, pulling it up with Him. The alternative hypothesis is not legend, nor exaggeration, nor the apparitions of a ghost. It is either lunacy or lies. Unless one can take the second alternative (and I can't) one turns to the Christian theory.

'What are we to make of Christ?' There is no question of what we can make of Him, it is entirely a question of what He intends to make of us. You must accept or reject the story.

The things He says are very different from what any other teacher has said. Others say, 'This is the truth about the universe. This is the way you ought to go,' but He says, '*I* am the Truth, and the Way, and the Life.' He says, 'No man can reach absolute reality, except through Me. Try to retain your own life and you will be inevitably ruined. Give yourself away and you will be saved.' He says, 'If you are ashamed of Me, if, when you hear this call, you turn the other way, I also will look the other way when I come again as God without disguise. If anything whatever is keeping you from God and from Me, whatever it is, throw it away. If it is your eye, pull it out. If it is your hand, cut it off. If you put yourself first you will be last. Come to Me everyone who is carrying a heavy load, I will set that right. Your sins, all of them, are wiped out, I can do that. I am Re-birth, I am Life. Eat Me, drink Me, I am your Food. And finally, do not be afraid, I have overcome the whole Universe.' That is the issue.

10

Must Our Image of God Go?
(1963)

The Bishop of Woolwich[1] will disturb most of us Christian laymen less than he anticipates. We have long abandoned belief in a God who sits on a throne in a localized Heaven. We call that belief anthropomorphism, and it was officially condemned before our time. There is something about this in Gibbon. I have never met any adult who replaced 'God up there' by 'God out there' in the sense 'spatially external to the universe'. If I said God is 'outside' or 'beyond' space-time, I should mean 'as Shakespeare is outside *The Tempest*'; i.e., its scenes and persons do not exhaust his being. We have always thought of God as being not only 'in' and 'above', but also 'below' us: as the depth of ground. We can imaginatively speak of 'Father in Heaven' yet also of the everlasting arms that are 'beneath'. We do not understand why the Bishop is so anxious to canonize the one image and forbid the other. We admit his freedom to use which he prefers. We claim our freedom to use both.

[1] This article, which first appeared in *The Observer* (24 March 1963), is a reply to the then Bishop of Woolwich, Dr J. A. T. Robinson's article 'Our Image of God Must Go', *The Observer* (17 March 1963), which is a summary of his book *Honest to God* (London, 1963).

His view of Jesus as a 'window' seems wholly orthodox ('he that hath seen me hath seen the Father').[2] Perhaps the real novelty is in the Bishop's doctrine about God. But we can't be certain, for here he is very obscure. He draws a sharp distinction between asking 'Does God exist as a person?' and asking whether ultimate reality is personal. But surely he who says yes to the second question has said yes to the first? Any entity describable without gross abuse of language as God must be ultimate reality, and if ultimate reality is personal, then God is personal. Does the Bishop mean that something which is not 'a person' could yet be 'personal'? Even this could be managed if 'not a person' were taken to mean 'a person and more' – as is provided for by the doctrine of the Trinity. But the Bishop does not mention this.

Thus, though sometimes puzzled, I am not shocked by his article. His heart, though perhaps in some danger of bigotry, is in the right place. If he has failed to communicate why the things he is saying move him so deeply as they obviously do, this may be primarily a literary failure. If I were briefed to defend his position I should say 'The image of the Earth-Mother gets in something which that of the Sky-Father leaves out. Religions of the Earth-Mother have hitherto been spiritually inferior to those of the Sky-Father, but, perhaps, it is now time to readmit some of their elements.' I shouldn't believe it very strongly, but some sort of case could be made out.

[2] John 14:9.

11

Priestesses in the Church?
(1948)

'I should like Balls infinitely better,' said Caroline Bingley, 'if they were carried on in a different manner ... It would surely be much more rational if conversation instead of dancing made the order of the day.' 'Much more rational, I dare say,' replied her brother, 'but it would not be near so much like a Ball.'[1] We are told that the lady was silenced: yet it could be maintained that Jane Austen has not allowed Bingley to put forward the full strength of his position. He ought to have replied with a *distinguo*. In one sense conversation is more rational for conversation may exercise the reason alone, dancing does not. But there is nothing irrational in exercising other powers than our reason. On certain occasions and for certain purposes the real irrationality is with those who will not do so. The man who would try to break a horse or write a poem or beget a child by pure syllogizing would be an irrational man; though at the same time syllogizing is in itself a more rational activity than the activities demanded by these achievements. It is rational not to reason, or

[1] *Pride and Prejudice*, ch. 11.

not to limit oneself to reason, in the wrong place; and the more rational a man is the better he knows this.

These remarks are not intended as a contribution to the criticism of *Pride and Prejudice*. They came into my head when I heard that the Church of England was being advised to declare women capable of Priests' Orders. I am, indeed, informed that such a proposal is very unlikely to be seriously considered by the authorities. To take such a revolutionary step at the present moment, to cut ourselves off from the Christian past and to widen the divisions between ourselves and other Churches by establishing an order of priestesses in our midst, would be an almost wanton degree of imprudence. And the Church of England herself would be torn in shreds by the operation. My concern with the proposal is of a more theoretical kind. The question involves something even deeper than a revolution in order.

I have every respect for those who wish women to be priestesses. I think they are sincere and pious and sensible people. Indeed, in a way they are too sensible. That is where my dissent from them resembles Bingley's dissent from his sister. I am tempted to say that the proposed arrangement would make us much more rational 'but not near so much like a Church'.

For at first sight all the rationality (in Caroline Bingley's sense) is on the side of the innovators. We are short of priests. We have discovered in one profession after another that women can do very well all sorts of things which were once supposed to be in the power of men alone. No one among those who dislike the proposal is maintaining that women are less capable than men of piety, zeal, learning and whatever else seems necessary for the pastoral office. What, then, except prejudice begotten by tradition, forbids us to draw on the huge reserves which could pour into the priesthood if women were here, as in so many other professions, put on the same footing as men? And against this flood of common sense, the opposers (many of them women) can produce at first nothing but an inarticulate distaste, a sense of discomfort which they themselves find it hard to analyse.

That this reaction does not spring from any contempt for women is, I think, plain from history. The Middle Ages carried their reverence for one Woman to a point at which the charge could plausibly be made that the Blessed Virgin became in their eyes almost 'a fourth Person of the Trinity'. But never, so far as I know, in all those ages was anything remotely resembling a sacerdotal office attributed to her. All salvation depends on the decision which she made in the words *Ecce ancilla*;[2] she is united in nine months' inconceivable intimacy with the eternal Word; she stands at the foot of the cross.[3] But she is absent both from the Last Supper[4] and from the descent of the Spirit at Pentecost.[5] Such is the record of Scripture. Nor can you daff it aside by saying that local and temporary conditions condemned women to silence and private life. There were female preachers. One man had four daughters who all 'prophesied', i.e., preached.[6] There were prophetesses even in Old Testament times. Prophetesses, not priestesses.

---

[2] After being told by the angel Gabriel that she has found favour with God and that she should bear the Christ Child, the Virgin exclaims 'Behold the handmaid of the Lord' (Luke 1:38). The *Magnificat* follows in verses 46–55.
[3] John 19:25.
[4] Matthew 26:26; Mark 14:22; Luke 22:19.
[5] Acts 2:1f.
[6] Acts 21:9.

At this point the common sensible reformer is apt to ask why, if women can preach, they cannot do all the rest of a priest's work. This question deepens the discomfort of my side. We begin to feel that what really divides us from our opponents is a difference between the meaning which they and we give to the word 'priest'. The more they speak (and speak truly) about the competence of women in administration, their tact and sympathy as advisers, their natural talent for 'visiting', the more we feel that the central thing is being forgotten. To us a priest is primarily a representative, a double representative, who represents us to God and God to us. Our very eyes teach us this in church. Sometimes the priest turns his back on us and faces the East – he speaks to God for us: sometimes he faces us and speaks to us for God. We have no objection to a woman doing the first: the whole difficulty is about the second. But why? Why should a woman not in this sense represent God? Certainly not because she is necessarily, or even probably, less holy or less charitable or stupider than a man. In that sense she may be as 'God-like' as a man; and a given woman much more so than a given man. The sense in which she cannot represent God will perhaps be plainer if we look at the thing the other way round.

Suppose the reformer stops saying that a good woman may be like God and begins saying that God is like a good woman. Suppose he says that we might just as well pray to 'Our Mother which art in Heaven' as to 'Our Father'. Suppose he suggests that the Incarnation might just as well have taken a female as a male form, and the Second Person of the Trinity be as well called the Daughter as the Son. Suppose, finally, that the mystical marriage were reversed, that the Church were the Bridegroom and Christ the Bride. All this, as it seems to me, is involved in the claim that a woman can represent God as a priest does.

Now it is surely the case that if all these supposals were ever carried into effect we should be embarked on a different religion. Goddesses have, of course, been worshipped: many religions have had priestesses. But they are religions quite different in character from Christianity. Common sense, disregarding the discomfort, or even the horror, which the idea of turning all our theological language into the feminine gender arouses in most Christians, will ask 'Why not? Since God is in fact not a biological being and has no sex, what can it matter whether we say *He* or *She*, *Father* or *Mother*, *Son* or *Daughter*?'

But Christians think that God Himself has taught us how to speak of Him. To say that it does not matter is to say either that all the masculine imagery is not inspired, is merely human in origin, or else that, though inspired, it is quite arbitrary and unessential. And this is surely intolerable: or, if tolerable, it is an argument not in favour of Christian priestesses but against Christianity. It is also surely based on a shallow view of imagery. Without drawing upon religion, we know from our poetical experience that image and apprehension cleave closer together than common sense is here prepared to admit; that a child who had been taught to pray to a Mother in Heaven would have a religious life radically different from that of a Christian child. And as image and apprehension are in an organic unity, so, for a Christian, are human body and human soul.

The innovators are really implying that sex is something superficial, irrelevant to the spiritual life. To say that men and women are equally eligible for a certain profession is to say that for the purposes of that profession their sex is irrelevant. We are, within that context, treating both as neuters. As the State grows more like a hive or an ant-hill it needs an increasing number of workers who can be treated as neuters. This may be inevitable for our secular life. But in our Christian life we must return to reality. There we are not homogeneous units, but different and complementary organs of a mystical body. Lady Nunburnholme has claimed that the equality of men and women is a Christian principle.[7] I do not remember the text in Scripture nor the Fathers, nor Hooker, nor the Prayer Book which asserts it; but that is not here my point. The point is that unless 'equal' means 'interchangeable', equality makes nothing for the priesthood of women. And the kind of equality which implies that the equals are interchangeable (like counters or identical machines) is, among humans, a legal fiction. It may be a useful legal fiction, but in church we turn our back on fictions. One of the ends for which sex was created was to symbolize to us the hidden things of God. One of the functions of human marriage is to express the nature of the union between Christ and the Church. We have no authority to take the living and seminal figures which God has painted on the canvas of our nature and shift them about as if they were mere geometrical figures.

This is what common sense will call 'mystical'. Exactly. The Church claims to be the bearer of a revelation. If that claim is false then we want not to make priestesses but to abolish priests. If it is true, then we would expect to find in the Church an element which unbelievers will call irrational and which believers will call suprarational. There ought to be something in it opaque to our reason though not contrary to it – as the facts of sex and

[7] Lady Nunburnholme, 'A petition to the Lambeth Conference', *Time and Tide*, vol. XXIX, No. 28 (10 July 1948), p. 720.

sense on the natural level are opaque. And that is the real issue. The Church of England can remain a church only if she retains this opaque element. If we abandon that, if we retain only what can be justified by standards of prudence and convenience at the bar of enlightened common sense, then we exchange revelation for that old wraith Natural Religion.

It is painful, being a man, to have to assert the privilege, or the burden, which Christianity lays upon my own sex. I am crushingly aware how inadequate most of us are, in our actual and historical individualities to fill the place prepared for us. But it is an old saying in the army that you salute the uniform, not the wearer. Only one wearing the masculine uniform can (provisionally, and till the *Parousia*)[8] represent the Lord to the Church: for we are all, corporately and individually, feminine to Him. We men may often make very bad priests. That is because we are insufficiently masculine. It is no cure to call in those who are not masculine at all. A given man may make a very bad husband; you cannot mend matters by trying to reverse the roles. He may make a bad male partner in a dance. The cure for that is that men should more diligently attend dancing classes; not that the ballroom should henceforward ignore distinctions of sex and treat all dancers as neuter. That would, of course, be eminently sensible, civilized, and enlightened, but, once more, 'not near so much like a ball'.

And this parallel between the Church and the ball is not so fanciful as some would think. The Church ought to be more like a ball than it is like a factory or a political party. Or, to speak more strictly, they are at the circumference and the Church at

[8] The future return of Christ in glory.

the centre and the ball comes in between. The factory and the political party are artificial creations – 'a breath can make them as a breath has made'. In them we are not dealing with human beings in their concrete entirety – only with 'hands' or voters. I am not of course using 'artificial' in any derogatory sense. Such artifices are necessary: but because they are our artifices we are free to shuffle, scrap and experiment as we please. But the ball exists to stylize something which is natural and which concerns human beings in their entirety – namely, courtship. We cannot shuffle or tamper so much. With the Church, we are farther in: for there we are dealing with male and female not merely as facts of nature but as the live and awful shadows of realities utterly beyond our control and largely beyond our direct knowledge. Or rather, we are not dealing with them but (as we shall soon learn if we meddle) they are dealing with us.

1) There is only ONE high
priest

Jesus Christ.
the church is female, this
includes men / women.

12

God in the Dock
(1948)

I have been asked to write about the difficulties which a man must face in trying to present the Christian Faith to modern unbelievers. That is too wide a subject for my capacity or even for the scope of an article. The difficulties vary as the audience varies. The audience may be of this or that nation, may be children or adults, learned or ignorant. My own experience is of English audiences only, and almost exclusively of adults. It has, in fact, been mostly of men (and women) serving in the RAF. This has meant that while very few of them have been learned in the academic sense of that word, a large number of them have had a smattering of elementary practical science, have been mechanics, electricians or wireless operators; for the rank and file of the RAF belong to what may almost be called 'the Intelligentsia of the Proletariat'. I have also talked to students at the Universities. These strict limitations in my experience must be kept in mind by the readers. How rash it would be to generalize from such an experience I myself discovered on the single occasion when I spoke to soldiers. It became at once clear to me that the level of intelligence in our army is very much lower than in the RAF and that quite a different approach was required.

The first thing I learned from addressing the RAF was that I had been mistaken in thinking materialism to be our only considerable adversary. Among the English 'Intelligentsia of the Proletariat', materialism is only one among many non-Christian creeds – Theosophy, spiritualism, British Israelitism, etc. England has, of course, always been the home of 'cranks'; I see no sign that they are diminishing. Consistent Marxism I very seldom met. Whether this is because it is very rare, or because men speaking in the presence of their officers concealed it, or because Marxists did not attend the meetings at which I spoke, I have no means of knowing. Even where Christianity was professed, it was often much tainted with Pantheistic elements. Strict and well-informed Christian statements, when they occurred at all, usually came from Roman Catholics or from members of extreme Protestant sects (e.g. Baptists). My student audiences shared, in a less degree, the theological vagueness I found in the RAF, but among them strict and well-informed statements came from Anglo-Catholics and Roman Catholics; seldom, if ever, from Dissenters. The various non-Christian religions mentioned above hardly appeared.

The next thing I learned from the RAF was that the English Proletariat is sceptical about History to a degree which academically educated persons can hardly imagine. This, indeed, seems to me to be far the widest cleavage between the learned and the unlearned. The educated man habitually, almost without noticing it, sees the present as something that grows out of a long perspective of centuries. In the minds of my RAF hearers this perspective simply did not exist. It seemed to me that they did not really believe that we have any reliable knowledge of historic man. But this was often curiously combined with a conviction that we knew a great deal about Pre-Historic Man: doubtless because Pre-Historic Man is labelled 'Science' (which is reliable) whereas Napoleon or Julius Caesar is labelled as 'History' (which is not). Thus a pseudo-scientific picture of the 'Caveman' and a picture of 'the Present' filled almost the whole of their imaginations; between these, there lay only a shadowy and unimportant region in which the phantasmal shapes of Roman soldiers, stage-coaches, pirates, knights in armour, highwaymen, etc., moved in a mist. I had supposed that if my hearers disbelieved the Gospels, they would do so because the Gospels recorded miracles. But my impression is that they disbelieved them simply because they dealt with events that happened a long time ago: that they would be almost as incredulous of the Battle of Actium as of the Resurrection – and for the same reason. Sometimes this scepticism was defended by the argument that all books before the invention of printing must have been copied and re-copied till the text was changed beyond recognition. And here came another surprise. When their historical scepticism took that rational form, it was sometimes easily allayed by the mere statement that there existed a 'science called textual criticism' which gave us a reasonable assurance that some ancient texts were accurate. This ready acceptance of the authority of specialists is significant, not only for its ingenuousness but also because it underlines a fact of which my experiences have on the whole convinced me; i.e., that very little of the opposition we meet is inspired by malice or suspicion. It is based on genuine doubt, and often on doubt that is reasonable in the state of the doubter's knowledge.

My third discovery is of a difficulty which I suspect to be more acute in England than elsewhere. I mean the difficulty occasioned by language. In all societies, no doubt, the speech of the vulgar differs from that of the learned. The English language with its double vocabulary (Latin and native), English manners (with their boundless indulgence to slang, even in polite circles) and English culture which allows nothing like the French Academy, make the gap unusually wide. There are almost two languages in this country. The man who wishes to speak to the uneducated in English must learn their language. It is not enough that he should abstain from using what he regards as 'hard words'. He must discover empirically what words exist in the language of his audience and what they mean in that language: e.g., that *potential* means not 'possible' but 'power', that *creature* means not 'creature', but 'animal', that *primitive* means 'rude' or 'clumsy', that rude means (often) 'scabrous', 'obscene', that the *Immaculate Conception* (except in the mouths of Roman Catholics) means the 'Virgin Birth'. A *being* means 'a personal being'. A man who said to me, 'I believe in the Holy Ghost, but I don't think it is a being,' meant: 'I believe there is such a Being, but that it is not personal.' On the other hand, *personal* sometimes means 'corporeal'. When an uneducated Englishman says that he believes 'in God, but not in a personal God', he may mean simply and solely that he is not an Anthropomorphist in the strict and original sense of that word. *Abstract* seems to have two meanings: (a) 'immaterial', (b) 'vague', obscure and unpractical. Thus Arithmetic is not, in their language, an 'abstract' science. *Practical* means often 'economic' or 'utilitarian'. *Morality* nearly always means 'chastity': thus in their language the sentence 'I do not say that this woman is immoral but I do say that she is a thief,' would not be nonsense, but would mean: 'She is chaste but dishonest.' *Christian* has an eulogistic rather than a descriptive sense: e.g., 'Christian standards' means simply 'high moral standards'. The proposition 'So and so is not a Christian' would only be taken to be a criticism of his behaviour, never to be merely a statement of his beliefs. It is also important to notice that what would seem to the learned to be the harder of two words may in fact, to the uneducated, be the easier. Thus it was recently proposed to emend a prayer used in the Church of England that magistrates 'may truly and indifferently administer justice' to 'may truly and impartially administer justice'. A country priest told me that his sexton understood and could accurately explain the meaning of 'indifferently' but had no idea of what 'impartially' meant.

The popular English language, then, simply has to be learned by him who would preach to the English: just as a missionary learns Bantu before preaching to the Bantus. This is the more necessary because once the lecture or discussion has begun, digressions on the meaning of words tend to bore uneducated audiences and even to awaken distrust. There is no subject in which they are less interested than Philology. Our problem is often simply one of translation. Every examination for ordinands ought to include a passage from some standard theological work for translation into the vernacular. The work is laborious but it is immediately rewarded. By trying to translate our doctrines into vulgar speech we discover how much we understand them ourselves. Our failure to translate may sometimes be due to our ignorance of the vernacular; much more often it exposes the fact that we do not exactly know what we mean.

Apart from this linguistic difficulty, the greatest barrier I have met is the almost total absence from the minds of my audience of any sense of sin. This has struck me more forcibly when I spoke to the RAF than when I spoke to students: whether (as I believe) the Proletariat is more self-righteous than other classes, or whether educated people are cleverer at concealing their pride, this creates for us a new situation. The early Christian preachers could assume in their hearers whether Jews, *Metuentes* or Pagans, a sense of guilt. (That this was common among Pagans is shown by the fact that Epicureanism and the Mystery Religions both claimed, though in different ways, to assuage it.) Thus the Christian message was in those days unmistakably the *Evangelium*, the Good News. It promised healing to those who knew they were sick. We have to convince our hearers of the unwelcome diagnosis before we can expect them to welcome the news of the remedy.

The ancient man approached God (or even the gods) as the accused person approaches his judge. For the modern man the roles are reversed. He is the judge: God is in the dock. He is quite a kindly judge: if God should have a reasonable defence for being the god who permits war, poverty and disease, he is ready to listen to it. The trial may even end in God's acquittal. But the important thing is that man is on the Bench and God in the Dock.

It is generally useless to try to combat this attitude, as older preachers did, by dwelling on sins like drunkenness and unchastity. The modern Proletariat is not drunken. As for fornication, contraceptives have made a profound difference. As long as this sin might socially ruin a girl by making her the mother of a bastard, most men recognized the sin against charity which it involved, and their consciences were often troubled by it. Now that it need have no such consequences, it is not, I think, generally felt to be a sin at all. My own experience suggests that if we can awake the conscience of our hearers at all, we must do so in quite different directions. We must talk of conceit, spite, jealousy, cowardice, meanness, etc. But I am very far from believing that I have found the solution of this problem.

Finally, I must add that my own work has suffered very much from the incurable intellectualism of my approach. The simple, emotional appeal ('Come to Jesus') is still often successful. But those who, like myself, lack the gift for making it, had better not attempt it.

13

We Have No 'Right to Happiness' (1963)

'After all,' said Clare, 'they had a right to happiness.'

We were discussing something that once happened in our own neighbourhood. Mr A. had deserted Mrs A. and got his divorce in order to marry Mrs B., who had likewise got her divorce in order to marry Mr A. And there was certainly no doubt that Mr A. and Mrs B. were very much in love with one another. If they continued to be in love, and if nothing went wrong with their health or their income, they might reasonably expect to be very happy.

It was equally clear that they were not happy with their old partners. Mrs B. had adored her husband at the outset. But then he got smashed up in the war. It was thought he had lost his virility, and it was known that he had lost his job. Life with him was no longer what Mrs B. had bargained for. Poor Mrs A., too. She had lost her looks – and all her liveliness. It might be true, as some said, that she consumed herself by bearing his children and nursing him through the long illness that overshadowed their earlier married life.

You mustn't, by the way, imagine that A. was the sort of man who nonchalantly threw a wife away like the peel of an orange he'd sucked dry. Her suicide was a terrible shock to him. We all knew this, for he told us so himself. 'But what could I do?' he said. 'A man has a right to happiness. I had to take my one chance when it came.'

I went away thinking about the concept of a 'right to happiness'.

At first this sounds to me as odd as the right to good luck. For I believe – whatever one school of moralists may say – that we depend for a very great deal of our happiness or misery on circumstances outside all human control. A right to happiness doesn't, for me, make much more sense than a right to be six feet tall, or to have a millionaire for your father, or to get good weather whenever you want to have a picnic.

I can understand a right as a freedom guaranteed me by the laws of the society I live in. Thus, I have a right to travel along the public roads because society gives me that freedom; that's what we mean by calling the roads 'public'. I call also understand a right as a claim guaranteed me by the laws, and correlative to an obligation on someone else's part. If I have a right to receive £100 from you, this is another way of saying that you have a duty to pay me £100. If the laws allow Mr A. to desert his wife and seduce his neighbour's wife, then, by definition, Mr A. has a legal right to do so, and we need bring in no talk about 'happiness'.

But of course that was not what Clare meant. She meant that he had not only a legal but a moral right to act as he did. In other words, Clare is – or would be if she thought it out – a classical moralist after the style of Thomas Aquinas, Grotius, Hooker and Locke. She believes that behind the laws of the state there is a Natural Law.

I agree with her. I hold this conception to be basic to all civilization. Without it, the actual laws of the state become an absolute, as in Hegel. They cannot be criticized because there is no norm against which they should be judged.

The ancestry of Clare's maxim, 'They have a right to happiness', is august. In words that are cherished by all civilized men, but especially by Americans, it has been laid down that one of the rights of man is a right to 'the pursuit of happiness'. And now we get to the real point.

What did the writers of that august declaration mean?

It is quite certain what they did not mean. They did not mean that man was entitled to pursue happiness by any and every means – including, say, murder, rape, robbery, treason and fraud. No society could be built on such a basis.

They meant 'to pursue happiness by all lawful means'; that is, by all means which the Law of Nature eternally sanctions and which the laws of the nation shall sanction.

Admittedly this seems at first to reduce their maxim to the tautology that men (in pursuit of happiness) have a right to do whatever they have a right to do. But tautologies, seen against their proper historical context, are not always barren tautologies. The declaration is primarily a denial of the political principles which long governed Europe: a challenge flung down to the Austrian and Russian empires, to England before the Reform Bills, to Bourbon France. It demands that whatever means of pursuing happiness are lawful for any should be lawful for all; that 'man', not men of some particular caste, class, status or religion, should be free to use them. In a century when this is being unsaid by nation after nation and party after party, let us not call it a barren tautology.

But the question as to what means are 'lawful' – what methods of pursuing happiness are either morally permissible by the Law of Nature or should be declared legally permissible by the legislature of a particular nation – remains exactly where it did. And on that question I disagree with Clare. I don't think it is obvious that people have the unlimited 'right to happiness' which she suggests.

For one thing, I believe that Clare, when she says 'happiness', means simply and solely 'sexual happiness'. Partly because women like Clare never use the word 'happiness' in any other sense. But also because I never heard Clare talk about the 'right' to any other kind. She was rather leftist in her politics, and would have been scandalized if anyone had defended the actions of a ruthless man-eating tycoon on the ground that his happiness consisted in making money and he was pursuing his happiness. She was also a rabid teetotaller; I never heard her excuse an alcoholic because he was happy when he was drunk.

A good many of Clare's friends, and especially her female friends, often felt – I've heard them say so – that their own happiness would be perceptibly increased by boxing her ears. I very much doubt if this would have brought her theory of a right to happiness into play.

Clare, in fact, is doing what the whole western world seems to me to have been doing for the last forty-odd years. When I was a youngster, all the progressive people were saying, 'Why all this prudery? Let us treat sex just as we treat all our other impulses.' I was simple-minded enough to believe they meant what they said. I have since discovered that they meant exactly the opposite. They meant that sex was to be treated as no other impulse in our nature has ever been treated by civilized people. All the others, we admit, have to be bridled. Absolute obedience to your instinct for self-preservation is what we call cowardice; to your acquisitive impulse, avarice. Even sleep must be resisted if you're a sentry. But every unkindness and breach of faith seems to be condoned provided that the object aimed at is 'four bare legs in a bed'.

It is like having a morality in which stealing fruit is considered wrong – unless you steal nectarines.

And if you protest against this view you are usually met with chatter about the legitimacy and beauty and sanctity of 'sex' and accused of harbouring some Puritan prejudice against it as something disreputable or shameful. I deny the charge. Foam-born Venus … golden Aphrodite … Our Lady of Cyprus … I never breathed a word against you. If I object to boys who steal my nectarines, must I be supposed to disapprove of nectarines in general? Or even of boys in general? It might, you know, be stealing that I disapproved of.

The real situation is skilfully concealed by saying that the question of Mr A.'s 'right' to desert his wife is one of 'sexual morality'. Robbing an orchard is not an offence against some special morality called 'fruit morality'. It is an offence against honesty. Mr A.'s action is an offence against good faith (to solemn promises), against gratitude (towards one to whom he was deeply indebted) and against common humanity.

Our sexual impulses are thus being put in a position of preposterous privilege. The sexual motive is taken to condone all sorts of behaviour which, if it had any other end in view, would be condemned as merciless, treacherous and unjust.

Now though I see no good reason for giving sex this privilege, I think I see a strong cause. It is this.

It is part of the nature of a strong erotic passion – as distinct from a transient fit of appetite – that it makes more towering promises than any other emotion. No doubt all our desires make promises, but not so impressively. To be in love involves the almost irresistible conviction that one will go on being in love until one dies, and that possession of the beloved will confer, not merely frequent ecstasies, but settled, fruitful, deep-rooted, life-long happiness. Hence *all* seems to be at stake. If we miss this chance we shall have lived in vain. At the very thought of such doom we sink into fathomless depths of self-pity.

Unfortunately these promises are found often to be quite untrue. Every experienced adult knows this to be so as regards all erotic passions (except the one he himself is feeling at the moment). We discount the world-without-end pretensions of our friends' amours easily enough. We know that such things sometimes last – and sometimes don't. And when they do last, this is not because they promised at the outset to do so. When two people achieve lasting happiness, this is not solely because they are great lovers but because they are also – I must put it crudely – good people; controlled, loyal, fair-minded, mutually adaptable people.

If we establish a 'right to (sexual) happiness' which supersedes all the ordinary rules of behaviour, we do so not because of what our passion shows itself to be in experience but because of what it professes to be while we are in the grip of it. Hence, while the bad behaviour is real and works miseries and degradations, the happiness which was the object of the behaviour turns out again and again to be illusory. Everyone (except Mr A. and Mrs B.) knows that Mr A. in a year or so may have the same reason for deserting his new wife as for deserting his old. He will feel again that all is at stake. He will see himself again as the great lover, and his pity for himself will exclude all pity for the woman.

Two further points remain.

One is this. A society in which conjugal infidelity is tolerated must always be in the long run a society adverse to women. Women, whatever a few male songs and satires may say to the contrary, are more naturally monogamous than men: it is a biological necessity. Where promiscuity prevails, they will therefore always be more often the victims than the culprits. Also, domestic happiness is more necessary to them than to us. And the quality by which they most easily hold a man, their beauty, decreases every year after they have come to maturity, but this does not happen to those qualities of personality – women don't really care twopence about our *looks* – by which we hold women. Thus in the ruthless war of promiscuity women are at a double disadvantage. They play for higher stakes and are also more likely to lose. I have no sympathy with moralists who frown at the increasing crudity of female provocativeness. These signs of desperate competition fill me with pity.

Secondly, though the 'right to happiness' is chiefly claimed for the sexual impulse, it seems to me impossible that the matter should stay there. The fatal principle, once allowed in that department, must sooner or later seep through our whole lives. We thus advance towards a state of society in which not only each man but every impulse in each man claims *carte blanche*. And then, though our technological skill may help us survive a little longer, our civilization will have died at heart, and will – one dare not even add 'unfortunately' – be swept away.